The Importance and Value of Older Employees

Anne Inga Hilsen · Dorothy Sutherland Olsen

The Importance and Value of Older Employees

Wise Workers in the Workplace

palgrave
macmillan

Anne Inga Hilsen
Fafo Institute for Labour
and Social Research
Oslo, Norway

Dorothy Sutherland Olsen
Nordic Institute for Studies in
Innovation, Research and Education
Oslo, Norway

ISBN 978-981-16-2860-3 ISBN 978-981-16-2861-0 (eBook)
https://doi.org/10.1007/978-981-16-2861-0

This Palgrave Macmillan imprint is published by the registered company Springer Nature Singapore Pte Ltd.
The registered company address is: 152 Beach Road, #21-01/04 Gateway East, Singapore 189721, Singapore

Preface

During our years as researchers we have amassed quite some experience on working life, learning at work and issues relating especially to seniors at work. One of the issues which employers and policymakers often emphasise is the importance of *active ageing* as if emphasising its importance were enough to make it happen. Our experience suggests that one of the ways to make active ageing a reality is to recognise and value seniors and what they bring to working life. A step towards this goal is to promote awareness of the potential and resources embodied in older employees. If age and experience make older workers valuable in working life, we need to understand how this "senior competence" is valuable. Our attempt to define senior competence, the competence that comes from long careers and high age, has moved us beyond conventional theories and discussions of competence, and into the field of wisdom. Involving older workers in describing and discussing what age and experience has contributed to in their daily work, has allowed us to capture and define a wide range of types of competence and practices that are dependent on both age and experience.

Conducting studies in several workplaces has also underscored the importance of relating competence to the specific job and workplace settings. Settings are necessary to understand senior competence. Only by exploring how older workers use their age and experience when performing their jobs in a particular work setting, can we discover what the advantages of senior competence are, both to the older workers themselves, their colleagues and their workplaces.

Oslo, Norway

Anne Inga Hilsen
Dorothy Sutherland Olsen

Acknowledgements

This book is based on research on older workers over a long time period and we are thankful to the following for funding this work:

The Research Council Norway Silver Lining project nr. 255210.

St. Olavs Hospital and KLP (Norway's largest pension company).

The Norwegian Labour Inspection Authority.

We are also grateful to Fafo Institute for Labour and Social Research and NIFU, the Nordic Institute for Studies in Innovation, Research and Education for supporting the work of writing this book.

Whenever working in the field of active ageing in Norway, Centre for Senior Policy (SSP) is always a staunch supporter, and we would like to thank them for engagement, feedback and useful discussions on earlier presentations of some of this work.

The main body of the interviews was carried out in cooperation with NAV Arbeidslivssenter Trøndelag (part of Norwegian Labour and Welfare Administration), and we would like to send particular thanks to Jon Sandvik and Britt Elin Strand for help and support during all group and plenary discussions.

We would also like to thank Trine Deichman Sørensen at Oslo Metropolitan University, who carried out some of the interviews and extend our thanks to all those who gave up their time to talk to us researchers and provide us with such rich and valuable material.

Contents

CHAPTER 1

Introduction

Abstract The aim of this book is to provide a better understanding of the value of older workers at work, and the importance of their contributions. Ageing populations have been studied in terms of the economic burden or the pressure on healthcare services and the rising numbers of seniors are generally viewed, more as a challenge, than an opportunity. However, in this book we are interested in viewing age as a potential benefit both for individuals and their workplaces.

Keywords Active ageing · Late career competence · Norway context

1.1 Introduction

"Why should we bother about older employees?" said a board member of a Norwegian hospital.

It is often difficult for managers to define the importance and value of older employees. Are they just necessary pairs of hands in an understaffed health service or are they key players in shaping and developing the workplace of today? After this board meeting, a manager felt she needed a better way to articulate the value and potential of older employees and any particular knowledge or contributions they could make. Based on this, the hospital initiated a research project with Norwegian social science research institutes.

A. I. Hilsen and D. S. Olsen, *The Importance and Value of Older Employees*, https://doi.org/10.1007/978-981-16-2861-0_1

The theme of the research in the Norwegian hospital is part of a greater social challenge facing many nations, that is the challenge of an ageing population. Ageing populations have been studied in terms of the economic burden or the pressure on healthcare services and the rising numbers of seniors are generally viewed, more as a challenge, than an opportunity. However, in this book we are more interested in viewing age as a potential benefit both for individuals and their workplaces. In addition to the hospital case, we will include data from other cases to gain a deeper understanding of the issues. We will examine the way in which senior employees actually use their knowledge and experience in their work and any advantages their age might give them.

The challenge of an ageing population is a challenge shared by most industrialised countries. The increase in life expectancy in combination with lower birth rates gives rise to a compositional shift from younger to older age groups. Across Europe there have been various research programmes investigating the challenge of an ageing population and looking at new ways of meeting this challenge. According to the EU Joint Programming Initiative (JPI) "More Years, Better Lives – The Potential and Challenges of Demographic Change" the challenge, seen from a policy perspective, has been described thus: "To sustain economic growth, prosperity and social development, many countries have recognised the need to increase the employment participation of people at higher working age. The degree of urgency is also reflected at all levels of the European policy agenda. The OECD views sustaining economic growth under conditions of population ageing by far as the most pressing global policy challenge for the next fifty years" (Hasselhorn & Apt, 2015: 12).

According to OECD (2019) the labour market participation for the age group 55–64 has increased by 8 percentage points over the last decade to an average of 64% in the OECD in 2018. Still "OECD countries are ageing rapidly. If no action is taken to improve the labour market situation of older workers, this could put a brake on further improvements in living standards and lead to unsustainable increases in social expenditures" (OECD, 2019: 9).

The demographic challenge has given rise to both research and policy efforts across most of Europe, as exemplified in the research programme JPI More Years, Better Lives—The Potential and Challenges of Demographic Change (Hasselhorn & Apt, 2015) that sums up where we have sufficient knowledge to act and where there are gaps in existing knowledge. The OECD report "Ageing and Employment Policies – Working Better with Age" sets out a wide range of policy recommendations centred around three broad areas: (1) Rewarding work and later retirement, (2) Encouraging employers to retain and hire older workers and (3) Promoting the employability of workers throughout their working lives. Of particular interest to the theme of our book is the first policy recommendation under theme three: promoting employability of workers throughout their working life. This recommendation is to "improve access to lifelong learning, especially for low-skilled and older workers; and better recognise skills acquired throughout working lives" (OECD, 2019: 17).

With increased life expectancy, age does not have to be regarded simply as a medical problem (Ilmarinen, 2006; Ilmarinen & Rantanen, 1999) or a challenge to welfare regimes. Active ageing regards experience and maturity as vital, resulting in skill and tacit knowledge, exercised by individuals and collectively, which are greatly valued by organisations (Hilsen & Ennals, 2005). Handled creatively, this group is potentially a new and unique resource.

In spite of extensive research arguing for the value and advantage of keeping older employees working longer, there is surprisingly little focus on why they are valuable. Vasconcelos (2018) argues that "their knowledge and expertise constitute an authentic source of wisdom capital that deserves careful attention from organizations to maintain by means of suitable incentives and training" (Ibid.: 114). He then goes on to stress the importance of training and motivation, but less about recognising what actually constitutes their existing knowledge and expertise.

The aim of this book is to provide a better understanding of the value of older workers, at work, and the importance of their contributions. The theme arises from the current challenges of ageing populations in western nations and the desire to keep employees actively involved in their work and contributing to society. Earlier research on cognitive ageing suggests that some abilities do decline with age; however, we subscribe to the idea that late career, i.e. from age 50 to 70 is not necessarily a period of stagnation or decline, but can also be a time for mastering new skills and finding new ways of using prior knowledge (Lahn, 2003). Our work builds on the idea that if employees continue to learn throughout their working career, then they will be in a better position to make an active contribution and hopefully choose to continue working rather than taking early retirement (Tikkanen et al., 2002).

The body of the work in this book is based on interviews with employees aged 50–70 and workplace studies carried out in large public sector institutions. We will provide in-depth descriptions of these studies and analyse them in terms of what they tell us about the competence of older employees. The analysis will compare findings with existing concepts of competence and discuss what characterises late career competence.

Our understanding of competence is based on the idea that, as well as formal education, learning occurs outside the classroom and in the workplace. Many of our subjects have worked for many years after the completion of formal education and we assume that they have continued to learn in their working situation. The basis of our understanding of learning is best described by the concept of situated learning. The concept of situated learning developed originally as a way of understanding learning occurring outside the classroom and was used by Lave and Wenger (1991) in their studies of apprentices to describe the way they learned at work. Since the first use of this concept, it has been widely used and developed in studies, largely of practice-based learning, where learning is embedded in activities carried out in the local environment. This concept has largely been used to study younger employees and how they develop knowledge and skills in the workplace during or after the completion of formal education. However, in this book we use this concept to study those who may have completed their formal education many years ago. Many of the earlier studies of adults learning at work are focused on knowledge developed in an occupational context and have been used largely to study adults from the phase when they move from education into employment and learning in the workplace, but few have placed particular emphasis on those over 50 (Lahn, 2003).

1.2 The Norwegian Context

The experiences of older employees described in this book are all based in Norway. As we assume the local and national context play an important role, we therefore include a short description of the situation in Norway with regard to adult learning and employment.

Norway has a limited workforce and traditionally low unemployment. This situation has doubtlessly influenced politicians, leading them to encourage elderly employees to continue working beyond the minimum retirement age. The employment rates of older workers have increased in Norway during the last 20 years, as in all the Nordic Countries. The employment rates, in percentages in the age group 55–64 in the years 2019/2000 respectively were: Norway 73/65, Denmark 72/56, Finland 67/42, Sweden 78/65, Iceland 81/84 and OECD total 62/48 (Source: OECD Employment database).

In 2011, Norway introduced a pension reform, aimed at achieving a more economically sustainable system while still promoting higher employment rates for older workers. To achieve this the insurance scheme introduced flexible retirement age and pension withdrawals between the ages of 62 and 75 years, based on cost neutrality. This means that early pension withdrawal results in a lower annual pension, and vice versa. At the same time, pension payments are not automatically dependent on income from work. Individuals are free to draw pension and continue working. Supplementary contractual pensions and occupational pensions are gradually being adapted to the reformed Norwegian National Insurance Scheme.

The pension reform is supposed to encourage employees to continue working after the minimum retirement age, at the same time the intention of the reform is that the decision to retire should not be purely an economic one. Employees must want to continue work and be healthy enough to do so. In addition, the employer must still have a need for their labour. As described by Midtsundstad and Nielsen (2019: 14): "The age limit for employment protection is important in this respect, as the employer can terminate the employment after this age without a justifiable basis. In other words, the decision of whether to continue working or not does not lie solely with the employee since the employer needs to grant approval. In 2015, the decision was made to raise the age limit for employment protection in Norway from 70 to 72 years, while the lowest permitted age limit was raised from 67 to 70 years. The goal of the change in legislation was to improve the freedom of choice for the oldest employees and, not least, to increase labour force participation among the over 67s".

Like most western nations, Norway has developed policies and plans for knowledge production. These plans and policies are designed to ensure that a modern western nation should have the necessary knowledge to staff public and private institutions and to be proactive in developing new businesses and contributing to research and innovation. Most of the activities linked to knowledge production have traditionally been aimed at educational establishments and to a lesser degree at other arenas in society where learning might take place. In 2018, Norway published a strategic policy document on competence. Unlike earlier documents, this one was not based on the idea that most education happens in educational institutions, but described a much broader group of learners in a wide social arena for learning. This strategy highlighted the importance of continued learning, lifelong learning, learning at work and informal learning, as well as formal learning in the education system. In a presentation of this strategy, the Norwegian prime minister referred to the continued participation of older citizens by saying that "nobody was past their sell-by date" and encouraging employees to continue to work beyond the minimum retirement age. Many activities followed in the wake of this document and committees were set up to look into the future competence needs and at further education. The reports from these committees confirm the need for lifelong learning and suggest a range of more flexible training initiatives more suitable for people in full-time employment. New funding has been allocated to collaborative projects between business and higher educational institutions and in particular to raise digital competence among employees (Kompetanse Norge, 2018). There is little doubt that recent policy shows an understanding of the importance of employees with work experience, however reference to seniors and their need for competence is mainly expressed as a desire to keep them in full-time employment as long as possible and ease the burden of pension costs.

Working life in Norway is characterised by close cooperation between employers, employee organisations and the welfare state. Regular dialogue and involvement of the different groups has become an integral part of working life is locally referred to as The Norwegian Model. This tradition of cooperation may improve the opportunities for seniors to be heard. (Dølvik et al., 2014). Norway also has a publicly funded organisation promoting the rights of older citizens, The Centre for Senior Policy (SSP). SSP act as a bridge builder between policymakers, academics, employers and employees and they carry out an annual survey of conditions for seniors. In the 2019 survey around half of employees over 50 reported that they had participated in some form of work-related training IPSOS (2019).

In spite of recent policy initiatives and cooperative traditions of the Norwegian workplace, studies of educational qualifications, literacy and numeracy in different age groups indicate that those over 50 have lower scores than those under 50. Data from the OECD Programme for the International Assessment of Adult Competencies (PIAAC) shows a clear decline in kills level in relation to age. According to PIAAC this decline in skills starts at around 35 and continues up to and beyond retirement.

Those over 50 also participate less in formal education or organised training, informal learning remains high throughout working life (Statistics Norway, 2018). The same study also revealed an age-related decline in employment i.e. 67% of people aged 55–66 are in employment while 18% of those over 66 are in employment.

In spite of policy declarations, these statistics present a picture which largely supports the stereotype of the older worker who is perhaps gradually withdrawing and not keeping up with the pace of change in society, however many of these over 50s who are apparently not participating in formal learning, are still active in the workplace. Are they just passively waiting for retirement? Do they have no value in the workplace?

References

Dølvik, J. E., Fløtten, T., Hippe, J. M., & Jordfall, B. (2014). *Den nordiske modellen mot 2030. Et nytt kapittel?* (Fafo-rapport 2014: 46). Fafo.

Hasselhorn, H. M, & Apt, W. (2015). *Understanding employment participation of older workers: Creating a knowledge base for future labour market challenges* (Research Report). Federal Ministry of Labour and Social Affairs (BMAS) and Federal Institute for Occupational Safety and Health (BAuA).

Hilsen, A. I., & Ennals, R. (2005). Age, mobility and knowledge: An action research approach. *AI & Society, 19*(4), 552–557.

Ilmarinen, J., & Rantanen, J. (1999). Promotion of work ability during ageing. *American Journal of Industrial Medicine, 1*, 21–23.

Ilmarinen, J. (2006). The ageing workforce: Challenges for occupational health. *Occupational Medicine, 56*(6). 362–364.

IPSOS. (2019). *Norsk seniorpolitisk barometer 2019*. www.ipsos.com/nb-no/norsk-seniorpolitisk-barometer-2019.

Kompetanse Norge. (2018). *EVU utvalget, Kunnskapsgrunnlaget Etter- og videreutdanning i Norge*.

Lahn, L.Ch. (2003). Competence and learning in late career. *European Educational Research Journal, 2*(1), 126–140.
Lave, J., & Wenger, E. (1991). *Situated learning: Legitmate peripheral participation*. Cambridge.
Midtsundstad, T., & Nielsen, R. A. (2019). *Heving av aldersgrensen for stillingsvern: Hvordan har virksomhetene og de ansatte tilpasset seg?* (Fafo-rapport 2019: 27). Fafo.
OECD. (2013). *Skilled for life?* OECD.
OECD. (2016). *Adult skills in focus: What does age have to do with skills proficiency?* OECD
OECD. (2019). *Working better with age, ageing and employment policies*. OECD Publishing. https://doi.org/10.1787/c4d4f66a-en.
Statistics Norway. (2018). https://www.ssb.no/utdanning/statistikker/lvm.
Tikkanen, T., Lahn, L.,Withnall, A., Ward, P., & Lyng, K. (2002). *Working life changes and training of older workers* (Research Report). Norwegian Institute of Adult Education.
Vasconcelos, A. F. (2018). Older workers as a source of wisdom capital: Broadening perspectives. *Revista de Gestão, 25*(1), 102–118. https://doi.org/10.1108/REGE-11-2017-002.

CHAPTER 2

Competence and Knowledge at Work

Abstract The theme of this book is long career competence in the workplace and competence of course includes a range of skills, ability and knowledge, which makes it possible for the individual to function and contribute in the workplace. What is considered appropriate competence will vary in different organisations and be dependent on the work, profession or tasks an employee is expected to carry out. The close link between competence and work means that it is not enough to simply know something; one must know how to carry out a task. There are many theories of knowledge and how competence is developed and used; here we focus on how competence and work-related knowledge have been conceptualised and how they have been used in relation to older employees. We include organisational knowledge, situated knowledge, professional knowledge and expertise and discuss how these concepts might be useful in understanding late career competence and older employees.

Keywords Organisational knowledge · Situated knowledge · Expertise · Professional knowledge · Competence · Older workers

A. I. Hilsen and D. S. Olsen, *The Importance and Value of Older Employees*, https://doi.org/10.1007/978-981-16-2861-0_2

2.1 Organisational Knowledge

A great deal of research on knowledge in work situations has been carried out by management scientists or economists with a desire to understand the value of organisations and how their human capital can be optimised. Different terms have evolved to describe knowledge such as tacit, explicit, procedural, dispersed or embedded, to name but a few. Knowledge is usually viewed as something owned by the organisation and something which has a value for the organisation. While researching this chapter we carried out searches of online databases for publications on organisational knowledge and learning. We found a large number of publications in the period up until 2005, however after that date there was a reduction in the number of publications on these themes and few notable attempts to develop theories which might be relevant for the age group in our studies. Some of the themes we found were related to knowledge sharing, knowledge networks and intra-professional knowledge as well themes related to culture and gender. We found that the more general findings on organisational knowledge and learning in the pre-2005 publications have frequently been incorporated into services provided by business consultants supporting HR and training managers. This suggests that many of the earlier findings have been accepted and we would expect to find them incorporated in working practice. We therefore chose to focus on the more classical works on organisational knowledge and use these studies to guide our work.

Metcalfe and Gibbons (1989) use the term knowledge base and they suggest that the knowledge base of an organisation is what defines the organisation. The way an organisation develops or acquires new knowledge, the way they articulate and enhance their knowledge is what gives the organisation its uniqueness and usually its competitive advantage. The idea of an organisation having a knowledge base is further developed by economists studying innovation such as Tidd et al. (2005) who describe the importance of "firm specific competences". The research done by Tidd et al. is based mainly on firms developing new technologies and they provide examples of firms developing theoretical knowledge based on their research and development work and developing practical knowledge from building and developing these technologies. Leonard (1998) discusses the development of firm-specific capabilities and the mechanisms which promote or hinder knowledge sharing and co-creation. Her theories have a lot in common with the concept of "core competencies" which was introduced by Prahalad and Hamel (1990), who describe these competencies as being the "collective learning of the organisation" and again highlight the importance of this knowledge in defining the position of the organisation in relation to competitors.

Other studies have developed the theme of organisational knowledge focusing on specific aspects. An example of this is the work focused more on knowing, rather than knowledge (Antonacopoulou, 2006). She attempts to avoid the limitations of viewing knowledge as an object separate from the context and processes which produced it. She proposes seven forms of knowing which are based on learning as problem-solving or "learning as a mystery". She distinguishes between hard technical knowledge and soft management knowledge and concludes with the following categories:

- Knowing by storing—when the emphasis is collecting relevant knowledge for a specific task.
- Knowing by repeating—when the emphasis is applying specific knowledge to similar situations.
- Knowing by improvising—when the emphasis is on exploring ways in which knowledge may be utilised in unfamiliar situations.
- Knowing by reflecting—when the emphasis is on the search for new meaning in relation to what is currently known.
- Knowing by questioning—when the emphasis is on assessing the relevance and applicability of knowledge in new situations and accepting ignorance.
- Knowing by synthesising—when the emphasis is on integrating what is known with what is discovered.
- Knowing by transforming—when the emphasis is on searching for a new platform of understanding.

(Ibid.: 26)

This way of focusing on knowing, rather than knowledge is interesting in terms of the current study of older employees particularly because it provides us with new ways of identifying learning based on the activities or ways of working described by workers themselves. This makes it possible to identify examples of learning which the learner may not be aware of.

Another thread of research which built on some of the ideas on organisational knowledge was the work of Lundvall and others who were interested in innovation and development of the knowledge economy. Lundvall was interested in how organisations use their knowledge to create economic growth. Lundvall was particularly interested in tacit knowledge and how firms and nation states could stimulate its development and then use it to create new products and services. Building on the studies of Ryles (1949), Lundvall developed a model of four knowledge types and a way of viewing the activities which are a prerequisite to developing these knowledge types.

- Know what
- Know why
- Know how
- Know who

(Lundvall, 1996: 5)

Know-what is based on learning facts, while know-why knowledge is an understanding of, for example, the laws of nature. Both these kinds of knowledge typically arise while undergoing formal education and the know-why kind of knowledge is predictably greater among those with a longer formal education. The know-how knowledge is usually based on practical experience, this kind of knowledge may be unique to the individual, but we would also expect to find it among groups of employees engaged in similar same activities, or those who have worked together in a project. The know-who kind of knowledge was the Lundvall's addition to earlier models and was the one that he viewed as being most important for innovation. Knowing *who* might know something which you don't know, knowing *who* has already done the task you are trying to do, knowing *who* has spoken or thought about the challenges you face. In all these examples the knowledge necessary to proceed can be gained in other ways than knowing who, however as Lundvall points out, knowing who and going directly to them is much faster. Lundvall sees this kind of knowledge as an integral part of working and existing in a modern technology-driven world.

Know-who and know-how are viewed as challenging for management as the skills necessary to know-who, to interact socially and absorb, share and embed new knowledge are not things which can be learned by going on a course. We understand a lot about practice-based knowledge, or know-how, however much of this knowledge is tacit and much of it arises when the learner is doing something else, i.e. not consciously learning. Therefore, neither employees nor employers may be aware of this kind of knowledge until the employee leaves and a gap suddenly appears. Not only are know-who and know-how challenging for management, but Lundvall also suggests that this kind of knowledge is dependent upon trust and requires, not only a network of useful contacts, but also the social skills to create and develop social networks. The concepts of know-who and know-how are particularly interesting with regard to the current study of older workers because both concepts implicitly assume a certain kind of pre-knowledge or experience that has been developed over time.

2.2 Situated Knowledge

While economists and management scientists were developing their own interpretations of organisational knowledge, studies of science and technology (STS) and feminist studies were developing some related concepts, one of these is situated knowledge. The concept of situated knowledge challenges the belief that there is any can kind of knowledge other than knowledge developed in situ and this of course challenges the value, or indeed the existence of knowledge derived from academic studies. Social studies of science and technology have questioned the objectivity of scientific knowledge and how we can understand objective knowledge without also accepting subjective interpretations.

Donna Harroway, a feminist researcher, was one of the first to draw attention to situated knowledge and it was in an attempt to provide a theory of objectivity (Thompson, 2015). Haroway (1998) wanted to step away from the traditional idea of knowledge as something separate from learning, to step away from the traditional idea of teacher and learner in a one-way dialogue and wanted instead to include learners, teachers or colleagues in an ongoing situation of knowledge production. As Thomson points out, it is common to view knowledge, at least scientific knowledge, as something universal no matter who possesses it, rather than something which has its real value in the *situation* where it was produced. Both Thomson and Harroway agree that scientific knowledge or impartial knowledge is dependent on the partiality of the local situation with its unique combination of persons and objects. This is also a theme developed by Knorr-Cetina (2003 [1999]).

An interesting aspect of situated learning is the concept of learning trajectories which stretch across space and time. In their analysis of situated learning, Lave and Wenger (1991) stress the importance of the gradual development of skills over time. They mention the learning opportunities provided by "the ongoing flow of reflective moments" (ibid.: 54) and how a variety of trajectories expose workers to different forms of participation in their tasks and transform them in different and unpredictable ways (ibid.: 19).

The concept of situated knowledge can be challenging for researchers studying older employees, because the concept does not deal with what happened before the situation in the same way as other concepts of knowledge. When discussing progression from newcomer to old-timer, the concept of situated knowledge emphasises the gradual development of identity rather than how the employee accesses a source of prior knowledge. Lave and Wenger (1991) describe this as moving from the periphery into the centre in terms of their trade. So, years spent on perfecting skills and performing tasks at work is a prerequisite to becoming an old-timer or a master craftsman, but there is less emphasis on the importance of formal or explicit knowledge. We might expect our older employees in the current study, to be masters of their roles at work, to be in the centre of their field. In terms of situated knowledge, we would expect that older employees would be understanding and interpreting their situation based on their own experiences either with the same employer or with multiple employers. We would expect older employees to have different views and understanding of historical events, of job descriptions, of formal procedures, of decisions taken, of strategies and of organisational changes depending on the situation now and the situation in the past. It is not certain that these understandings and interpretations will differ radically from those of younger employees, indeed the differences might not be identified by researchers who do not get an in-depth understanding of the situation and the interviewee's interpretations of it. By asking older employees to share their experiences of situations and how they reacted to them, we can gain useful information about what they bring to these situations in terms of experience and what they learn from these situations.

2.3 Expertise and Professional Knowledge

Many years of research have been devoted to the theme of expertise and how experts or professionals work. Here we consider the findings of some of these researchers, such as, Collins and Evans, Eraut and the Dreyfus brothers. Since professional status and expertise require an extended period of time to develop and master, we thought that these concepts might be relevant to our understanding of older workers and their competence.

As with the other studies reviewed in this chapter, it is often difficult to separate concepts of knowledge or competence from the process of developing this knowledge or competence. Dreyfus and Dreyfus (1986) is an example of this. They developed a model of skills acquisition which describes the stepwise changes a novice must progress through to become an expert. The model consists of five discrete steps from novice, through advanced beginner, competent and proficient to expert. One of the main features of the model of skills acquisition is that the learner begins by learning the facts and carefully following the rules, as the novice progresses, more activities are carried out in a swift, intuitive way. While this model might well work when explaining how one learns to dance a tango, it has been criticised because of its limitations. One of the limitations is the kind the problem the employee is dealing with, if it is a simple problem, such as *should I change gear in the car?*, then we do see that experienced drivers act in an swift and intuitive way, however if you are trying to communicate new laws or regulations and their consequences for employers, then you require more than a swift intuitive answer. One must be able to interpret the listener, has he or she understood? Then consider rephrasing the information and communicating it in a new way. This is only one example, but it suggests that when the issue is more complex and cannot simply be memorised, that it will require a combination of intuition and conscious evaluation. For example, the delicate balance between tacit and explicit knowledge necessary for a medical practitioner to make a diagnosis does not fit easily into the model. The increasing importance of tacit knowledge and intuitive nature of the actions of many experts makes this model interesting, however there is more to senior competence than simply tacit knowledge and intuition.

Collins and Evans (2009) have observed a change in the way in which expertise has been understood, "a move away from seeing knowledge and ability as quasi logical or mathematical and toward a more wisdom-based or competence-based model" (ibid.: 23). In their periodic table of expertise Collins and Evans (ibid.: 14) present a matrix of knowledge associated with experts and non-experts. This model is quite complex with different levels and many sub-divisions, here we mention the most important types of knowledge and competence, thereafter we select the subcategories which might be affected by age or by having a long working career.

Collins and Evans distinguish between a knowledge of facts, which can be taught and learned, like how to move the bishop on a chess board and specialist tacit knowledge, which can only be gained by immersion in a field over a longer period of time. This tacit knowledge is further defined as including contributory expertise "which is what you need to do an activity with competence" (ibid.: 14) or internalised physical skills. The stages for developing this kind of skill, are similar to the model developed by Dreyfus and Dreyfus. The other kind of tacit knowledge which we would expect experts to exhibit is interactional knowledge which is "the ability to master the language of a specialist domain" (ibid.). Collins and Evans are particularly interested in this kind of expertise, because they claim that it has largely been ignored by academics and the focus has traditionally been on tacit or explicit knowledge. They describe interactional knowledge as more informal, than formal, however they suggest that this kind of knowledge can be developed without the expert having practice-based experience. It can be developed through dialogue with experts. They mention how journalists develop this kind of knowledge, or academics writing reviews on the work of others, also salespersons and managers typically develop interactional knowledge.

Collins and Evans point out that long experience alone is not equivalent to developing expertise, so we cannot assume that our older employees will all be more knowledgeable than their younger colleagues by sheer dint of being their longer. Experts are people who have used their long careers to develop skills. We may however expect some of our senior employees to have developed their skills in such a way that they have a high level of contributory knowledge or that they have mastered the language of their domain or have developed their interactional knowledge.

Professionals are often defined as a group of particular interest with regard to their competence and how it is developed. Most professions have their own formal education and training and indeed the body of theoretical knowledge linked to the profession is often central to the very existence of the profession itself. In his studies on developing professional knowledge, Eraut (1994, 2000) confirms the importance of formal education and training and mentions the importance of an understanding of shared knowledge, approved by the profession. However, in addition to all the formal training and understanding of theoretical knowledge, many professionals must also learn from practical experience. He points out the importance of prior examples of similar situations and how these experiences are regularly used to take decisions. Although many of the examples a professional will call upon will be from the professionals' own experience, much will also be learned from the reported experiences of others. The latter may be learned in a formal situation, such as lawyers and doctors studying documentation of previous cases, or they may be learned informally by exchanging experiences with colleagues (Eraut, 1994: 46). By learning from past experiences, it is possible for the expert to refine his or her understanding of which procedures and actions from previous examples will be most appropriate in the current situation. Eraut (ibid.) suggests that a semi-conscious patterning may take place, which makes it difficult for the professional to recognise or at least articulate the pattern which is being used. Learning from experience, is not simply living through the experience, but could occur when one consciously reflects upon an action. Focusing on an experienced action many times, as this action is repeated during a professional career, might result in a range of different meanings being generated from this action depending on the meaning, context and the moment (ibid.: 104). Much of what is learned from experience will not be the result of conscious learning, but might happen while the professional is doing something else and when learning is the last thing on her mind. Again this kind of learning is not something which can be completed during the first year of practicing a profession and suggests implicitly that older professionals and younger professionals may have very different competence and while both groups may have a similar relationship to theoretical knowledge, their relationship to practical knowledge will be different.

When analysed more closely, Eraut (2000) suggests that professional knowledge consists of:

- A combination of routine procedures
- Proficiency in these routines
- Ability to handle non-routine situations

The ability to solve well-defined and ill-defined problems and to continuously develop new problem-solving strategies is important in order to be able to be an expert in one's profession. As Eraut points out, most professions consider the amateur as a person who tries to apply tried and tested solutions without engaging in the problem at hand and considering if there are perhaps multiple solutions to the problem and selecting the most appropriate. Problem-solving is addressed in formal professional training, however solving problems which are not easily described is usually learned from practical experience and therefore the expert is expected to have worked long enough in order to gain the experience necessary to develop these skills. As well as problem-solving skills, Eraut (ibid.) mentions communication, ability to work in teams and an understanding of ethics in practice as examples of competence which is important to most professions and which is not routinely taught in formal education or training courses.

2.4 Competence, Knowledge and Seniors

In this chapter we have presented some of the more traditional theories of organisational knowledge and learning at work. There is of course a large body of literature on career development at work. Much of the research on career development is indeed relevant in the context of lifelong learning; however, we have not included this literature. Questions about career development did not arise in our interactions with older employees although they did mention job mobility, which we will discuss later.

This brief overview of how knowledge at work has been conceptualised gives us an interesting starting point for understanding the kind of knowledge or competence which older employees might be talking about when we interview them. It also gives us an idea of the importance which different actors have attributed to different kinds of work-based knowledge. It is evident from these studies that the theme of age is not considered relevant in many of the better-known concepts of knowledge, however there is an underlying assumption of experience. This experience does not simply arise from elapsed time, but from time spent on a variety of tasks and overcoming challenges. Some of the concepts of knowledge discussed here and the methods used to identify knowledge and learning have helped us to formulate some of our interview questions and to interpret and understand our findings. We did however also want to consider research aimed more specifically at understanding age and older employees and this is described in the next chapter.

References

Antonacopoulou, E. (2006). Modes of knowing in practice: The relationship between knowledge and learning revisited. In B. Renzl, K. Matzler, & H. Hinterhuber (Eds.), *The future of knowledge management*.

Collins, H., & Evans, R. (2009). *Re-thinking expertise*. The University of Chicago Press.

Dreyfus, H. L., & Dreyfus, S. E. (1986). *Mind over machine: The power of human intuition and expertise in the era of the computer*. Basil Blackwell.

Eraut, M. (1994). *Developing professional knowledge and competence*.

Eraut, M. (2000). Non-formal learning and professional knowledge at work. *British Journal of Educational Psychology, 70*(1), 113–136.

Haroway, D. (1998). Situated knowledges: The science question in feminism and the privilege of partial perspectivce. *Feminist studies, 14*(3), 575–599.

Knorr-Cetina, K. (2003 [1999]). *Epistemic cultures: How the sciences make knowledge*. Harvard University Press. (Third printing 2003).

Lave, J., & Wenger, E. (1991). *Situated learning legitmate peripheral participation*. Cambridge University Press.

Leonard, D. (1998). *Wellsprings of knowledge*. Harvard Business School Press.

Lundvall, B. Å. (1996). *The social dimension of the learning economy* (DRUID Working Papers 96-1). DRUID, Copenhagen Business School, Department of Industrial Economics and Strategy/Aalborg University, Department of Business Studies.

Metcalfe, G. S., & Gibbons, M. (1989). Technology, variety and organisation: A systematic perspective on the competitive process. *Research on Technological Innovation Management and Policy, 4*, 153–193.

Prahalad, C. K., & Hamel, G. (1990, May–June). The core competence of the corporation. *Harvard Business Review*, pp. 79–90.

Ryles, G. (1949). *The concept of Mind*. Penguin.

Thompson, C. M. (2015). Situated knowledge, feminist and science and technology studies perspectives. *International Encyclopedia of the Social and Behavioral Sciences, 22*, 1–4.

Tidd, J., Bessant, J., & Pavitt, K. (2005). *Managing innovation* (3rd ed.). Wiley.

CHAPTER 3

What Do We Know About the Knowledge of Older Workers?

Abstract In this chapter we give a brief presentation of relevant findings on senior competence and learning abilities from national and international studies. We include studies which have tried to assess the knowledge of older employees, studies which consider the abilities and potential of older employees to continue to develop their knowledge and studies which address the value or advantages of having knowledgeable older employees.

Keywords Senior competence · Learning abilities · Knowledgeable older workers

Earlier research on learning and competence in relation to age has been focused on different themes. The themes relevant to the current study are those discussing the knowledge or competence which older employees demonstrate, but we are also interested in studies of the abilities or the potential of older employees to continue to develop this knowledge. The studies we review here are roughly divided into those, which examine the relationship between formal education and the knowledge of older workers, and those studies more interested in learning after the completion of formal education. Lastly, we look at those studies attempting to

A. I. Hilsen and D. S. Olsen, *The Importance and Value of Older Employees*, https://doi.org/10.1007/978-981-16-2861-0_3

understand if there is a particular kind of knowledge, which is characteristic of older workers, and attempting to describe the value of such knowledge for employees and employers.

3.1 Education and the Skills of Older Workers

Many of the studies on the relationship between age and knowledge have been focused on education and how it affects the abilities and the performance of older workers. The results of large national and international studies on workers are publicly available and one of these is the OECD Programme for the International Assessment of Adult Competencies (PIAAC). This programme studies competence and participation of employees in learning activities in over 40 countries and is carried out every 5 years. The study includes a questionnaire and interviews and a practical assessment of skills in literacy, numeracy and problem-solving. One of the conclusions is that many employees over 55 have fewer years of formal education than their younger colleagues. This is perhaps not so surprising when we think of how the opportunities for education have developed during the last 30 or 40 years and how policymakers have increased their interest in the role of education in our modern societies. The study does find a positive link between higher education or a long formal education and the continued participation of older employees in the workplace. The study found a gradual reduction in the numbers of employees participating in further education or organised training courses at work after the age of 35, however the opportunity for continued learning throughout working life was found to have positive effect on older workers and their ability to remain active at work. The importance of learning outside formal education, i.e. either practice-based work experience or experience gained outside work was also found to be increasingly important for older employees (OECD, 2016). Practical tests of skills revealed a gradual decline in all skills (literacy, numeracy and problem-solving) from the age of 30. It has been suggested that adults who continue to use their skills have a lower risk of losing them (OECD, 2016: 3). In many countries, the gap between the skills levels of employees and the requirements of their employment varied and in some countries the gap was much less for older employees, than for their younger colleagues. Although the proficiency of older workers is considered lower (OECD, 2016), their productivity is no lower than younger workers. Qualitative studies have also found that the productivity of older workers remains high, although there was variation depending on the workplace. The EU project "Working Life Changes and the Training of Older Workers" (WORKTOW) found a varied situation where older workers were less active in some areas, but participating as actively as their younger colleagues in others (Tikkanen et al., 2002). They found that older employees participated in informal and non-formal training in the same way as younger workers, but to a lesser extent in formal training.

Other studies have provided information on the effects of participation of older adults in some forms of training for improved literacy skills, based on the International Adult Literacy Survey with a Dutch supplement (van der Kamp & Boudard, 2003). Desjardins and Warnke (2012) have provided an overview of age-skill profiles and potential factors influencing skill gain and skill loss at both individual and population levels. "Although the evidence regarding the age-related decline of cognitive skills is widespread and the explanation that this may be part of 'normal ageing' is intuitively appealing, it is not possible regardless of research design to identify whether ageing effects are caused by neurological maturation effects, behavioural and practice effects, or the interaction of these with contextual effects. Moreover, there is some evidence to suggest that there are several factors that can mitigate, delay or prevent the cognitive decline that is associated with so called 'normal ageing'. Education, training, and a number of physical, social and mental activities have all been implicated as possible factors which help to mitigate the age-related decline in cognitive skills" (ibid.: 55).

Some studies have also found evidence of the pressure on older workers to continue learning. An example of this is an analysis of the retirement decision of Norwegian governmental employees, based on survey data (retrospective cohort data), which found that one out of four claimed that their retirement was related to employers' demands for more education (Midtsundstad, 2005). This perceived competence gap is affecting older employees, as shown by Midtsundstad, who found that older employees experiencing a mismatch between actual competence and competence needed to perform current work tasks had a significantly higher probability of leaving the labour market early.

3.2 Can Older Employees Learn New Things at Work?

There are different ways of finding out if older workers are continuing to learn as they age. One can look at how often they participate in formal education or other forms of organised learning. One can also ask managers and younger colleagues about the performance of older employees or one can carry out more explorative studies and find out what older employees actually do at work, and look for examples of learning which the employees or employers may not be aware of. Here we review some studies which attempt to say something about older employees continued learning.

A number of surveys, including in Norway, document that older workers do indeed participate in vocational training, however they participate less frequently than their younger colleagues (Hagen & Skule, 2001; Skaalvik et al., 2000; Wiborg et al., 2011). The reasons for this are probably many and complex. Some of the explanation is related to the level of education. The general level of education is higher among younger than among older workers, and persons with a high formal education participate more in post- and further education than persons with low formal education. However, even when comparing groups with equal educational attainment, we see that older workers participate less in competence development than those who are younger, even when comparing groups with the same level of education. There must therefore also be other explanations for older people participating less in competence development.

This information on participation in organised adult learning, confirms that there is a potential for older employees to continue their learning after completing their formal education and although there are fewer actively participating in this form of learning, than in younger ages groups, we assume that those who complete courses have learned something from them.

As mentioned in the PIAAC study (OECD, 2016) learning outside formal education is important for older workers, who have perhaps been working for many years, since completing their formal education. Their modern workplaces have probably changed considerably since 55-year-olds left full-time education. Modern workplaces are frequently reorganised, new roles come and go and technology is continuously being updated and renewed. If older workers are to remain active at work, they will almost certainly have to learn new things and develop new skills.

A number of studies are interested in the learning that goes on at work and highlight the importance of participation and learning opportunities in the workplace (van den Heuvel et al., 2006). European experiences of lifelong learning and older workers have been studied by Tikkanen and Nyhan (2006). They view ageing as "a lifelong learning and developmental process" (ibid.: 10) and maintain that new challenges at work, which match the employee's interests are necessary to promote continuous learning. Therefore, they conclude that adult learning should be understood broadly including education, training and "participative collective workplace learning". They find that older workers can indeed continue to learn, however this ability will be affected by the kind of workplace they have as well as how employers value the knowledge and experience of older workers and support them in their tasks. The intentions and proactivity, or agency, of the older workers are seen as important if older employees are to continue learning (Billitt & van Woerkom, 2006).

Some studies have found that opportunities for older employees to learn, are much greater in large organisations and may, as already noted, they can be exposed to a greater degree of training and skills development than in small and medium enterprises (SMEs) (McNair et al., 2004); this might be an important factor determining their ability and willingness to remain active at work. The skills base of older workers, as nurtured by the organisational context, is crucial in developing what Hirsch (2005) refers to as "sustainable working lives". Other studies have found that organisational change is also an important source of learning for employees who have experienced them several times. Fuller and Unwin found that workers who had to adapt to a new situation and a new form of organisation had indeed gained useful insights and developed ways of working which they were able to use again later (Fuller & Unwin, 2006: 268).

Some studies have found examples of employees who are dealing with change and are indeed learning new skills. A study of opportunities for lifelong learning at work in Norway included some interesting descriptions of what employees and their managers think of seniors and their ability to develop their competence and participate in the workplace (Becken et al., 2015). They found that there were good opportunities for older employees to continue to develop their competence, but in practice, it was very much up to the individuals to take the initiative. When it is up to individuals, we see that motivation is important. There were of course examples of many older employees who wanted to prioritise time at home with older partners or with grandchildren, but there were many examples where employees had changed their minds when they found something which motivated them at work.

One example was a nurse who was exhausted and had various ailments due to many years of hard physical work. She had decided to take early retirement as soon as possible. In the meantime, her manager offered her a new position, which was less physically demanding, but challenging in other ways. She was invited to establish a new department responsible for competence development for nurses in the region. This new position required that the nurse had to master new skills, absorb a lot of new information and develop new procedures. She was very unsure about taking the position, but decided to try, and when interviewed she had been doing the new job for some time. She had decided to postpone retirement and carry on working. She said she loved her job, had learned so much and was so glad to have had the opportunity to learn something new, do something different and to take responsibility for something important.

In another example, a public sector employee who found the IT system for registering all his working tasks far too difficult to master and said he was looking forward to retirement and leaving all the bureaucracy behind. Just as the interviewers were leaving, he surprised them by saying there was actually one thing that might make him stay on at work and that was a new IT system for mapping public property. It turned out that this employee was the international super-user for this IT system. He was in frequent contact with the system developers, suggesting changes and improvements to the software and, much to his wife's dismay, accepted calls from users all around the world, offering them help at any time day or night. If he could be allowed to work on this system and not bother with all the bureaucracy, he would definitely consider working a few more years.

These are interesting examples of how older employees might be tempted to withdraw and participate less in certain situations and even retire early. However, in both situations, alternative responsibilities and tasks resulted in these employees being stimulated to learn new things and to participate actively. These examples support the findings of the other studies mentioned earlier, that there is a great variety in the type of learning that works for older employees.

3.3 Senior Competence

Many authors have written about competence and working knowledge, but fewer have mentioned older workers. Here we consider literature and earlier studies on the competence and working knowledge of older workers and ask if there is such a thing as senior competence. It is not always the seniors themselves, who can say most about their competence, but employers have something to say on the theme, as was found by Bo Göranzon (1990), who carried out research on how employers value the competence of senior workers. He found that some managers are aware of the competence of seniors and judge it to be valuable for their firms. When asked to describe it, they say it is different from the kind of theoretical knowledge, which is easily identifiable in younger employees straight out of schools and universities. Some seniors do have theoretical knowledge, but what most of them have, is a kind of practical knowledge acquired through experience. Göranzon (ibid.) argues that the practical and tacit knowledge of experienced workers is a necessary resource for good productivity. He differentiates between three types of knowledge: *Propositional or theoretical knowledge*, *Skills, or practical knowledge* and *Knowledge of familiarity*. (Göranzon et al., 2006: 192). Whereas *theoretical knowledge* can be acquired through books, or replaced by computers, *skills* need practical experience and *familiarity* is the integrated knowledge developed over time in a community of practice.

Göranzon (1990) makes a point of discussing how computers, or artificial intelligence, may replace some work operations, although basically operations following known rules and theoretical knowledge. As artificial intelligence (AI) develops, this may change as computers are able to acquire skills through repeated performance and feedback. Familiarity takes not only experience over time, but the "knowledge we gain by exchanging experience with colleagues and fellow-workers" (ibid.). Familiarity is social in its being, developed not only through one's own practice but through sharing stories of this experience with others. Familiarity is inspired by Wittgenstein (1953/2001) and his claim that a concept gets its meaning through its use, which is in dialogue with others. "The meaning of a word is its use in the language" (PI §43). In On Certainty (Wittgenstein, 1969) elaborates on the social aspect of knowledge. "If experience is the ground of our certainty, then naturally it is past experience. And it isn't for example just my experience, but other's people's, that I get knowledge from" (On Certainty §275). If this type of knowledge (familiarity) is dependent on taking theoretical knowledge into practice and sharing the emerging knowledge with others, it depends on both experience and time. Even if Wittgenstein does not relate his discussion to age, it is obvious that age and experience are somewhat related. More years, more experience, and therefore more occasions for developing knowledge of all three types.

Göranzon is also primarily concerned with knowledge development, unrelated to age as such. His examples of theoretical knowledge, practical knowledge and familiarity use examples of a boat builder and a photographer (Göranzon, 2006: 13–16) and two cases of forest evaluation and social insurance (Göranzon, 1990). His cases demonstrate how knowledge (skills and familiarity) is developed over time in a community of practice and goes far beyond theoretical knowledge. Göranzon does not specifically use the concept of *community of practice*, but it is this particularly social aspect of knowledge development that is described in the concept of familiarity.

Community of practice is a concept first proposed by Jean Lave and Etienne Wenger in their book Situated Learning (Lave & Wenger, 1991). Although they suggested the concept *community of practice* they are clear that they describe a phenomenon that has existed for as long as people have been learning and sharing their experiences. "Communities of practice are formed by people who engage in a process of collective learning in a shared domain of human endeavour: a tribe learning to survive, a band of artists seeking new forms of expression, a group of engineers working on similar problems, a clique of pupils defining their identity in the school, a network of surgeons exploring novel techniques, a gathering of first-time managers helping each other cope" (Wenger-Trayner, 2015). Community of practice is relevant to the type of learning that depends on working with others, as Göranozon's discussion of skills and familiarity (1990, 2006).

Learning together and developing knowledge that is more extensive than that of the single members of the community makes the concept of familiarity relevant to our discussion of the type of competence developed by older workers through long careers and many years in working life.

We would expect that workplaces with a mix of older and younger employees would provide opportunities for different age groups to learn from one another. By combing the competence of younger workers with newly acquired theoretical knowledge and the competence of older, experienced workers, we would expect that new combined knowledge might develop. Hilsen and Ennals (2007) describe an example of this process in their study of a good practice model for organisational learning and experience sharing across age divides and distances. The model consisted of both a digital flow chart that described the progress in a field of executive work, as well as a dialogical process of experience sharing. They chose to call the tool "The Golden Link", in recognition of the value of linking seniors, juniors and information technology. The experienced senior gave a detailed and step-by-step description of the progress of a task, while the junior with better computer skills filled out the flow chart. It was developed locally in a Norwegian enterprise facing an increasing number of employees approaching retirement age, and also facing the challenge of how to make the experience-based knowledge and competence of these older workers available to the organisation and to younger colleagues with less experience. Similar examples are found in (Olsen & Børing, 2019), where employers deliberately used shadowing techniques to transfer knowledge from seniors to juniors. The model was a tool not only to support cross-generational communication and learning, but also to enable access for mobile workers to the knowledge of experienced seniors not physically present.

The ability to use new technology at work is becoming increasingly important in the modern workplace and this prompts the question of whether older workers actually have more or less digital competence than their younger colleagues. Attitudes towards older workers strongly suggest that they are perceived as less competent than younger colleagues (OsloEconomics, 2018: 44). If they are seen as less competent, they may be challenged less frequently, given fewer opportunities to develop skills or even be excused from mastering the new tools. Also there are huge individual differences, based on (among others) personality, exposure to technology and type of work. Even if younger people are more comfortable with digital technology, this may be a cohort phenomenon rather than a result of ageing. Growing up in a digital world gives a different experience than being introduced to it as grown-ups, as exemplified in Tapscott's (1998, 2009) concept of the Net Generation or Prensky's

(2001) concept of Digital Natives and Digital Immigrants. This would imply that when the Net Generation grows older, they will continue to be comfortable with the technology. Experience with the tasks to be carried out might also compensate for unfamiliarity with the digital tools to be used.

A recent study (Soja & Soja, 2020) on getting older employees to use ICT in an efficient way included an overview of the advantages of older employees (in this case over 50). Their paper is based on a review of literature on older employees and ICT and 187 interviews with employees involved in the recent implementation of ICT systems. Some of these advantages were related to loyalty and lower absenteeism, however most of them were related to skills or knowledge based on long experience. Some of these advantages were:

- Know-how and experience, ability to comprehend the whole
- Awareness of one's own limitations and strong points, self-confidence
- Greater soft skills (e.g. interpersonal skills)
- Reason in solving problems
- Reason in dealing with co-workers and clients (Soja & Soja, 2020: 411).

The authors conclude that older employees have the potential to develop skills which they see as being complementary to ICT and as such these skills could be very valuable in a technology-rich environment. They mention skills such as communication with co-workers and clients, problem-solving and the ability to develop good plans. Activities relating to planning and implementing ICT systems are all enhanced when older employees with their advanced interpersonal skills use their ability to facilitate adaptation (ibid.: 427).

Age differences and learning abilities in a work life context is a complex phenomenon and needs to be addressed in a contextual way (Lahn, 2003: 130). Even psychological tests (such as IQ tests or the Rorschach test) show individual differentiated results. A Norwegian longitudinal study followed a group of 100 individuals from the age of 13 in 1939 into their 70s with repeated tests at the age of 13, 58 and 68 years of age (Seim, 1988, 1997 in Daatland & Solem, 2011: 77). Some individuals scored higher with age, others lower, some personal traits differed, but also differed between individuals of the same age.

In a review of the literature on cognitive ageing and learning abilities in an occupational context, Lahn (2003) claims that “multidimensional and non-linear perspectives are increasingly replacing models of late career as a period of declining expertise” (ibid.: 126). This is supported by the results from the WORKTOW project. Age seems to be a poor predictor of performance, both personal performance and work performance (Lahn, 2003: 128; OsloEconomics, 2018: 28).

In spite of age being a poor predictor of performance at the individual level, there are studies that relate performance to age at an aggregated level. A study using meta-analytic techniques (number of samples = 92) to determine the patterns of mean-level change in personality traits across the life course on personality and age uses the personality test The Big Five. This test measures scores on five major dimensions of personality: Openness, Conscientiousness, Extraversion, Agreeableness and Neuroticism. The study concludes that as one ages, Neuroticism is reduced and so is Extraversion, Agreeableness and Conscientiousness increases and Openness rises early in life but declines with age (OsloEconomics, 2018: 34; Roberts et al., 2006). As we shall see from our interviewees who talk about different approaches to work as they age, and the personality traits from the Big Five may be relevant in discussion of such changes.

Like the PIAAC findings mentioned earlier, Solem also finds in this review that there is “no general decline in work performance with age” (Solem, 2007: 32), mainly because of individual differences in the effect of ageing. Solem quotes the gerontologist Dannefer (2003 in Solem, 2007: 15) who has called this process of increased individual differences «cumulative advantage/disadvantage». As one grows older, age is only one factor that influences work performance, alongside a wide range of other individual and institutional factors.

To summarise, we can say that there is evidence that employees over 50 do indeed continue to participate in formal education and organised courses, however they do this to a lesser extent than their younger colleagues. With regard to informal learning there are also examples where employees have either chosen, been encouraged or even forced to learn new skills, to master new ways of working or to deepen their understanding in order to keep their jobs or meet the challenges presented at work. The few researchers who have broached the theme of the elusive senior competence have mentioned various nuances such as familiarity

(Göranzon, 2006) and soft skills linked to implementing new technologies (Soja & Soja, 2020). This leaves us with some unanswered questions such as why do fewer older employees participate in formal training and organised courses? Several of the studies reviewed so far have mentioned the importance of informal learning, why do we know so little about the informal learning of older employees at work? Lastly is the issue of the value of this senior competence; the studies presented here suggest that management decisions vary greatly and that many may be based on long-held beliefs about older employees or old age in general. We will attempt to shed some light on some of these questions later, but in the next chapter we will present our methods for gathering and analysing our empirical data from older employees at work.

References

Becken, L. E., Carlsten, T. C., Børing, P., Wedde, E., Olsen, D. S., & Berg, H. (2015). *Livslang læring og ansettbarhet for arbeidstakere over 55 år*. [Lifelong learning and employability among employees 50+]. Proba samfunnsanalyse.

Billett, S., & van Woerkom, M. (2006). Older workers and learning through work: The need for agency and critical reflection. In Tikkanen, T., & Nyhan, B. (Eds.), *Promoting lifelong learning for older workers: An international overview* (pp. 177–189). Office for official Publications of the European Communities.

Daatland, S. O., & Solem, P. E. (2011). *Aldring og samfunn* (2.ed.). Fagbokforlaget.

Dannefer, D. (2003). Cumulative Advantage/Disadvantage and the Life Course: Cross-Fertilizing Age and Social Science Theory. *The Journals of Gerontology: Series B, 58*(6), November 2003, Pages S327–S337. https://doi.org/10.1093/geronb/58.6.S327.

Desjardins, R., & Warnke, A. (2012). *Ageing and skills: A review and analysis of skill gain and skill loss over the lifespan and over time*. OECD Education Working Papers, No. 72. Paris: OECD Publishing. https://doi.org/10.1787/5k9csvw87ckh-en.

Fuller, A., & Unwin, L. (2006). Older workers' learning in changing workplace contexts: barriers and opportunities. In T. Tikkanen & B. Nyhan (Eds.), *Promoting lifelong learning for older workers: An international overview* (pp. 258–270). Office for Official Publications of the European Communities.

Göranzon, B., Hammarén, M., & Ennals, R. (Eds.). (2006). *Dialogue, skill and tacit knowledge*. John Wiley.

Göranzon, B. (1990). *Det praktiska intellektet*. Carlsson Bokförlag.

Hagen, A., & Skule, S. (2001). *Yrke, opplæringsbehov og interesse for etter- og videreutdanning*. Fafo-rapport 372.
Hagen, A., og Skule, S. (2007). Den norske modellen og utviklingen av kunnskapssamfunnet. In I. Dølvik, J. E. m.fl. (red.), *Hamskifte. Den norske modellen i endring* (s. 145–168). Gyldendal Norsk Forlag.
Hilsen, A. I., & Ennals, R. (2007). Virtual links: Intergenerational learning and experience sharing across age divides and distances. In AI & Society. https://doi.org/10.1007/s00146-007-0166-6 (published before print).
Hirsch, D. (2005). *Sustaining working lives: A framework for policy and practice.* Joseph Rowntree Foundation.
Lahn, L. Ch. (2003). Competence and learning in late career. *European Educational Research Journal, 2*(1), 126–140.
Lave, J., & Wenger, E. (1991). *Situated learning: Legitmate peripheral participation.* Cambridge.
McNair, S., Flynn, M., Owen, L., Humphreys, C., & Woodfield, S. (2004). *Changing work in later life: A study of job transitions.* University of Surrey, Centre for Research into the Older Workforce.
Midtsundstad, T. (2005). *Ikke nødvendigvis sliten... En analyse av tidligpensjonering og seniorpolitikk i staten.* Fafo-report 482. Oslo: Fafo.
OECD. (2016). *The survey of adult skills. Reader's companion* (2nd ed). OECD Skills Studies. OECD Publishing. https://doi.org/10.1787/9789264258075-en.
Olsen, D., & Børing, P. (2019). Kompetanseutvikling og livslang læring blant seniorer innenfor akademikeryrker. *NIFU Report, 2019*, 14.
OsloEconomics. (2018). *Aldringens betydning for helse, arbeidskapasitet og arbeidsprestasjoner.* Rapport utarbeidet på oppdrag fra Senter for seniorpolitikk. 2018_32. Oslo: OsloEconomics.
Prensky, M. (2001). Digital natives, digital immigrants. *On the Horizon, 9*(5), 1–6.
Roberts, B. W., Walton, K. E., & Viechtbauer, W. (2006). Patterns of mean-level change in personality traits across the life course: A meta-analysis of longitudinal studies. *Psychological Bulletin, 132*(1), 1–25.
Skaalvik, E. M. m.fl. (2000). *Voksenopplæring i Norge ved tusenårsskiftet. Deltakelse, motivasjon og barrierer.* Norsk voksenpedagogisk forskningsinstitutt.
Soja, E., & Soja, P. (2020). Fostering ICT use by older workers: Lessons from perceptions of barriers to enterprise system adoption. *Journal of Enterprise Information Management, 2*(33), 407–434.
Solem, P. E. (2007). Seniorer i arbeidslivet. Kunnskap om aldring og arbeid. Norsk institutt for forskning om oppvekst, velferd og aldring. NOVA Rapport 16/2007. Oslo: NOVA.

Tapscott, D. (1998). *Growing up digital: The rise of the net generation*. McGraw-Hill.
Tapscott, D. (2009). *Grown up digital: How the net generation is changing your world*. McGraw-Hill.
Tikkanen, T. Lahn, L. C., Withnall, A., Ward, P., & Lyng, K. (2002). *Working life changes and training of older workers*. Research Report. VOX & European Commission ISBN: 82-7724-039-2.
Tikkanen, T., & Nyhan, B (Eds.). (2006). *Promoting lifelong learning for older workers: An international overview*. Cedefop Reference series. Luxembourg: Office for Official Publications of the European Communities.
van der Kamp, M., & Boudard, E. (2003). Literacy proficiency of older adults. *International Journal of Educational Research, 39*(3), 253–263.
Van den Heuvel, J. (2006). Board roles in small and medium-sized family businesses: Performance and importance. *Corporate Governance, 14*(5), 467–485.
Wenger-Trayner, E. & B. (2015). *Introduction to communities of practice: A brief overview of the concept and its uses*. https://wenger-trayner.com/introduction-to-communities-of-practice/.
Wiborg, Ø., Sandven, T., & Skule, S. (2011). *Livslang læring i norsk arbeidsliv 2003–2010*. Trender og resultater fra Lærevilkårsmonitoren. NIFU Rapport 5/2011.
Wittgenstein, L. (1953/2001). *Philosophical investigations*. The German Text with a Revised English Translation. Blackwell.
Wittgenstein, L. (1969). On certainty (Uber Gewissheit). In G. E. M. Anscombe & G. H. von Wright (Eds.). Translated by Denis Paul and G. E. M. Anscombe. Basil Blackwell, 1969–1975. http://budni.by.ru/oncertainty.html.

CHAPTER 4

Research Design

Abstract In this chapter we will present the research design and explain the methods used to select, gather and analyse data. The empirical data for this exploration is based on findings from two case studies: One in a large Norwegian hospital and the other in Government agency. In addition, we will draw on data from a project in another Government organisation, a state department, where some of the same questions about age and competence were asked.

Keywords Research design · Case study · Qualitative interviews · Older workers

We view the research process as an evolving process, whereby we as researchers are having our assumptions challenged again and again as new data becomes available and new ideas and understandings emerge. Each time we are challenged, this causes us to revisit these assumptions and refine them based on the empirical evidence and our interpretations of this evidence. Our choice of research theme lends itself to an explorative approach where we hope to develop theory or concepts rather than test hypothesis.

Research based on qualitative methods is often criticised for being overly descriptive, however in situations where concepts are not well understood, there is a need for good descriptions. We do, however agree

A. I. Hilsen and D. S. Olsen, *The Importance and Value of Older Employees*, https://doi.org/10.1007/978-981-16-2861-0_4

with the critics who suggest that description alone is seldom enough to make a scientific contribution and this has led us to use a systematic way of gathering data, developing descriptions, analysing these descriptions and developing new concepts. In this way, we intend to develop, not theory, but a systematic concept of the older worker related to their experience and their know-how. Our methods of conceptual ordering of data and the systematic documentation of relationships between themes and concepts are inspired by Strauss and Corbin and their work on grounded theory (Strauss & Corbin, 1998).

4.1 Research Methods

The empirical data for this explorative study comes from two case studies, a hospital and an Inspectorate, in the public sector in Norway. The case studies were chosen in organisations with a large number of older employees and where management was interested in supporting older employees in their work and achievements. Thus these cases are in no way representative of all Norwegian workplaces or even the public sector. They are instead chosen because of the opportunity for us to learn from detailed descriptions of the work experience of older workers in these organisations. Another reason for choosing these particular cases is that the researchers were given access to a large number of employees over a period of time. The number of case studies was limited in order to study the experiences of different employees in the same context and to make the context an integral part of the study. There are many factors which can influence the experiences of workers and affect how they and their colleagues view their competence. It has therefore been important for us to view the events and situations described in our data in the context of the organisations where they happen.

4.2 Data and Data Collection

The data comes largely from interviews and is supplemented by written documents such as annual reports and strategy documents as well as online sources and local media reporting. Most of the data was collected using individual face-to-face interviews, group interviews and plenary discussions at larger more formal gatherings of employees.

Interviews are the chosen method of many researchers and there are different kinds of interviews. Kvale (1996: 5) suggests the aim of the interview is "to obtain descriptions of the life world of the interviewee with respect to interpreting the meaning of the described phenomena", this matches well with our aims, where we want to find alternative conceptions of meaning and reality in the local context. We are not interested in quantifying objective data, but would rather interpret meaningful events and relations in the lived world of the interviewee. The most common form of interview is the individual interview, which can be conducted as a kind of conversation, allowing the voice of the interviewee to be heard. This kind of interview is usually steered with an interview guide; in the current study a semi-structured interview guide was developed. This method of interviewing allows the interviewee to choose much more of the content of the interview and also gives them space to describe things in more detail and sometimes to think out loud. This way of interviewing has the advantage that the interviewees' perceptions of their everyday life can be brought into focus.

When asking individuals about what they know, what they do at work and what value this might have, it is often difficult to get good data without individuals editing it. Interviewees are often concerned that the interview should sound good, maybe that it should fit in with what their employer wants to hear, or that it should match what they want to hear about their own careers. This does not mean that people have been untruthful in interviews, but answers to questions do not always provide the best and most interesting information for researchers. Therefore, we have endeavoured to provide space for people to tell their stories. In our own experience and supported by others (Kvale, 1996), we have found that interview subjects get more taken up with the narrative, trying to describe it the way it was and they often stop to correct themselves as they remember more details of recent events. It is then up to the researcher to analyse this rich data.

As well as the individual interview, data was gathered in group interviews. The individual voices do not always get heard so well in these interviews, but they can often generate very fast interactions which build upon each other. Participants are frequently stimulated by what colleagues say, correct them and elaborate on what they have said. This kind of interview is often more challenging for the interviewer, but usually very rewarding.

In the hospital study, 8 individual interviews were carried out, in addition to seminars with small-group discussions with 2–8 participants and plenary discussion where the smaller groups presented their results and the other groups were invited to supplement, comment and add their own results. There were 3 seminars a year with approx. 50 participants each time, covering a total of up to 450 older employees over a 3-year period. The individual interviews lasted from 1 to 1½ hours and the group sessions for around 2 hours.

In the Inspectorate we carried out two group interviews with 4 participants from two regional offices, one group interview with 8 participants at the Directorate level, 6 individual interviews as well as group discussions in smaller groups and plenary with 42 participants representing the whole organisation (Directorate and regional offices). One group interview and two individual interviews were conducted online in the data meeting room of the Inspectorate. The rest were conducted face-to-face.

The supplementary cases from another project were based on 11 individual interviews in a government department.

4.3 The Cases

One is in a large regional hospital in Mid-Norway, integrated with the Norwegian University of Science and Technology. They have a staff of approximately 10,500, of whom roughly 2400 are 55 years or older. The employees consulted were mostly nurses and auxiliaries, but also some doctors and other hospital staff.

The second case was a government agency, with 600 employees, organised with a central office—the Directorate, 7 regional offices and 16 local offices throughout the country. The Directorate regulates the agency's overall strategy, programmes and information. The district offices guide and supervise individual enterprises in local communities. They have administrative, supervisory and information responsibilities in compliance with the requirements of the Working Environment Act. This case is referred to as the Inspectorate.

4.4 How the Data Was Analysed

The individual interviews were recorded and transcribed, the group interviews were recorded and written notes were produced. Notes were taken in the larger discussion groups. In group interviews and larger discussion groups, there was more than one researcher present.

By allowing interviewees to tell their stories, one inevitably ends up with lots of unstructured text, lots of digressions and lots of examples of situations which are important for interviewees. Unlike structured interviews where we compare the different answers to questions, we wanted to take advantage of the rich data, so, inspired by grounded theory (Glaser & Strauss, 1967; Strauss & Corbin, 1998), we have proceeded through several iterations of categorising themes and concepts, then structuring relationships between them.

4.5 Grounded Theory

Grounded theory was first developed in the 60s by Glaser and Strauss, their intention was to develop theory directly derived from data. The idea is that theory developed in this way will bear closer resemblance to reality than other more abstract theories. The ideas of Glaser and Strauss have been developed and refined in subsequent years. This method for gathering and analysing data is based on a systematic process of data gathering, followed by iterative analysis and categorisation. This method is relevant in situations where the researcher does not begin with a preconceived theory in mind and is not striving to test a theory. The method is appropriate for researchers who start with an area of study and want to build theory by allowing it to emerge from the data (Strauss & Corbin, 1998: 13). Categorising or grouping of themes in an iterative process allows for the consideration of alternative meanings and interpretation of phenomena. Based on the categories identified in the first stage of analysis, the building blocks for the next stage will emerge.

Grounded theory has, of course, been criticised and one of the criticisms is that, like many qualitative methods, findings cannot be generalised. However, the aim of grounded theory is to develop what Corbin and Straus call "representative concepts" "ultimately to build a theoretical explanation by specifying phenomena, in terms of the conditions that give rise to them, how they are expressed through action/interaction, the consequences that result and the variation of these" (Strauss & Corbin, 1990: 421). It is therefore important that researchers using grounded theory include the conditions and context which are associated with the phenomenon found in the particular data. Anyone trying to reproduce the study would have to ensure that conditions and context were the same.

4.5.1 *First Stage*

Rough grouping of pieces of text. These can be sentences or paragraphs in a longer narrative, or they can be direct answers to questions. This is a process of sorting and labelling. This first grouping is quite general but the process becomes more rigorous by using various analytical tools. These tools can be.

Checking the perceived meaning of the statement with the context. There are often multiple interpretations of statements and it is important that the statements do not take on a life of their own, independent of their context.

Comparing statements with the researchers' previous experience is a way of sensitising the researcher to the choice of category. Comparing with previous examples can support the choice of category, but also reveal less obvious aspects of the statement.

Questioning different aspects of the concept, turning it around. This questioning can be done with the interviewee, between multiple researchers or by one researcher alone asking critical questions.

Avoiding standard ways of thinking about the phenomenon. This reduces the risk of the researcher closing themselves off from potential new interpretations and understanding.

4.5.2 *Second Stage*

This is where one tests the labels and regroups. One can test the labels with the interviewees, but in some cases the labels might not be easily recognisable to interviewees. Reading and re-reading transcripts and re-listening to recordings is normal in this phase and the researcher should question the reasons for grouping and again look for alternatives. If the same words are used by different interviewees, then at this stage it is normal to question whether they refer to the same or a similar phenomenon or event. It is here that we dig deeper and consider different potential meanings, different dimensions and interpretations. It is not just a case of counting how many interviewees refer to the same phenomenon, or how many describe it the same way, but what are the similarities and what are the different nuances in their words and in the actions behind the words. We also define subcategories and re-group data under multiple categories. Hopefully by this stage some of the earlier labels emerge strengthened and perhaps some have merged and others have appeared from within the same data. It is during this stage that one starts to move from labels to concepts. As Strauss and Corbin (1998) emphasise, a concept is "an abstract representation of an event, object, or action/interaction that a researcher identifies as being significant in the data" (ibid.: 103). These concepts may arise directly from the terminology of the interviewees, their own words, or they may be based on the meaning they evoke for the researcher.

4.5.3 *Third Stage*

At this stage the theory building becomes more evident and one moves from fragmented labels to related categories. Here we look for relationships, not necessarily causality, but more in terms of conditions. It should be possible to develop some statements based on the data and it is in this phase that one looks for one main category to express the findings.

Grounded theory is a powerful tool to analyse and identify emerging new theory or concepts. At the same time there are some difficulties in claiming to use grounded theory, or being inspired by it, as we claim. George Allan (2003) reflects on several of these difficulties, with which we sympathise. Firstly, he argues that "Glaser and Strauss' (1967) emphasis on the researcher having 'no preconceived ideas' when collecting and analysing data" (Allan, 2003: 8) is difficult from two perspectives. Firstly, how do you get participants to agree to something vague and not well described? To this, we would like to add the question, how do you ensure informed consent from participants who don't know what the study is about? Secondly, how do you code the material, how do you know if a statement is of importance, if you have no preconceived ideas of what to look for?

In our case(es) we started looking for something which we didn't have a clear understanding of, namely what does late career competence actually look like in a workplace setting. Over many years as researchers we had come across several stories that had made us curious and given us glimpses of what the competence of older workers could look like or how might be described. During a project in an industrial plant someone mentioned that the older production workers could "hear when something was off kilter before the alarm went off" by the sound of the machines. We were reminded of this story when, in our hospital case, the nurses talked about *the clinical eye*. This experience-based, integrated knowledge takes years to develop, but can obviously emerge in many different settings.

Allan (ibid.) also discusses the difficulties of when you have found enough, how do you know you have reached the point of *saturation*, with reference to Glaser (1978). Do you ever reach a point of saturation or is there always more to find if you keep looking and continue the analysis? For us this was a very relevant point, as the material is extensive and rich, and could potentially always reveal more. All the individual interviews are taped, and tone of voice, laughter or similar expressions might also be analysed. Allan (ibid.: 9) argues that instead of looking for this point of saturation, "the theory could be allowed to emerge right from the start. I use the term 'allowed to emerge' to mean that concepts and categories should be noted and considered as soon as they are noticed and this is the start of the theory".

4.6 How This Method Was Used in the Current Project

The phenomenon being investigated was what older employees know and how they use what they know to contribute to their workplace. We were keen to avoid a listing up of qualifications and courses attended by employees, therefore we deliberately chose a less conventional way of discussing competence. We did not mention formal, informal or non-formal competence, nor did we ask about education or skills. To articulate the practical use of late career competence, we asked about practice and practical situations where the older worker thought that he or she had an advantage over younger colleagues with shorter careers.

In order to gain a better understanding of this phenomenon and to stimulate interviewees to share their experiences and their thoughts with us, two main questions were asked:

> "In what ways have you found your age and the length of your career to be an advantage in the performing of your job?"

> "In what ways are older employees with and long careers more proficient at their jobs than their younger colleagues?"

Thus the first categories shaping the data collection, were: age, career and advantage.

In spite of the way these pre-chosen categories steered the data collection, a rich variety of descriptions of working practice and specific events arose from the interviews. Our job was then to analyse the data and develop categories through a bottom-up data-driven analysis. In the first round of analysis, we looked for the main statements which provided answers to the original questions. We then began to group these statements and label them.

Certain phases emerged which required more clarification. These were mainly terms used to describe some kind of competence which the interviewees considered important. One example was *the clinical eye*. In order to better understand this term and how it was used, we asked "what does the clinical eye see?", "what is different between the clinical eye and the ordinary eye?".

Another term frequently used without any explanations or indications of its characteristics was "life experience". We asked for examples, but also "how does one use life experience?".

A term used by several was to have been on stormy seas before (in Norwegian: "har vært ute en vinternatt før", having been out in a winter night before). This phase is well known and most interviewees would not consider it necessary to explain what is meant by it. It was important for us to find out what lay behind it for our interviewees. So we asked "What does an employee who has been on rough seas before, do differently from a younger employee?".

In the next stage of analysis findings from small-group discussions were presented in plenary sessions to larger groups of fellow employees, who were invited to comment. This resulted in some corrections, some more details on some points and suggestions for additional themes to be included. After this round of scrutiny and refinement by the employees themselves, the process took on a more structured form and some follow-up questions which arose.

Initially we asked how older employees contribute more than less experienced colleagues? This was followed up with questions on the novel contributions of younger employees and how these can be used by the older employees. We asked how older and younger colleagues together might contribute to each other's learning. Discussions on the question of how older employees contribute did not focus exclusively on length of service or on experience, but also produced rich descriptions on how age and experience is useful, not only for the employees, but also for their employer.

At this stage we developed subcategories relating to career, age and advantage, basically using terms as they were used by the interviewees.

After this stage of refining categories and developing subcategories, we moved over to phase where we tried to gain a better understanding of what the categories were telling us. We did this by drawing upon the researchers' experience and the experiences of others who have researched seniors at work, or development of competence at work. Here we found that many of the experiences recounted were similar to those described in connection with practice learning among novices (Dreyfuss & Dreyfuss, 1986) and the gradual development of apprentices (Lave & Wenger, 1991). We also found similarities with Eraut's (1994) findings on professionals, but we also found examples of competence, skills or abilities which do not match with earlier findings. This phase of analysis led us to question whether there is a term we could use to describe the kind of competence these older employees are telling us about. Our understanding of this kind of competence, developed from the ideas of senior competence as described by Göranzon (1990, 2006) in Chapter 3 and evolved through our analysis of the data until we ended up with the concept of *the wise worker*, which is presented and discussed in Chapter 7.

References

Allan, G. (2003). A critique of using grounded theory as a research method. *The Electronic Journal of Business Research Methods (EJBRM)*. http://www.ejbrm.com/.

Dreyfuss, S. E., & Dreyfuss, H. L. (1986). *Mind over Machine*. Free Press.

Eraut, M. (1994). *Developing professional knowledge and competence*. The Falmer Press.

Glaser, B. (1978). *Theoretical sensitivity: Advances in the methodology of grounded theory*. Sociology Press.

Glaser, B., & Strauss, A. (1967). *The discovery of grounded theory: Strategies for qualitative research*. Aldine.

Göranzon, B., Hammarén, M., & Ennals, R. (Eds.). (2006). *Dialogue, skill and Tacit knowledge*. Wiley.

Göranzon, B. (1990). *Det praktiska intellektet*. Carlsson Bokförlag.

Kvale, S. (1996). *InterViews: An introduction to qualitative research interviewing*. Sage.

Lave, J., & Wenger, E. (1991). *Situated learning legitimate peripheral participation*. Cambridge University Press.

Strauss, A., & Corbin, J. M. (1990). *Basics of qualitative research: Grounded theory procedures and techniques.* Sage.
Strauss, A., & Corbin, J. (1998). *Basics of qualitative research: Techniques and procedures for developing grounded theory* (2nd ed.). Sage.

CHAPTER 5

Over 50s at Work: Findings from Case Studies

Abstract In this chapter we present the findings from individual and group interviews. We have tried to adhere as much as possible to their descriptions, examples and terms in the following. The data comes largely from interviews, and most of the data was collected using individual face-to-face interviews, group interviews and plenary discussions at larger more formal gatherings of employees. In these interviews and discussions participants were asked to reflect on their own competence and how they perceive the long career competence of older workers in their specific workplaces.

Keywords Interviews · Reflections · Examples

In this chapter, we present the findings from our case studies, illustrating how the interviewees describe the advantages of long work careers, and age in the workplace.

Engaging older workers and encouraging them to talk about their competence and how they view their own contribution to the workplace, has allowed us to capture and define a wide range of competences.

The empirical material is generated largely through the questions "In what ways have you found your age and the length of your career to be an advantage in the performing of your job?" and "In what ways are older employees with long careers more proficient at their jobs than their

A. I. Hilsen and D. S. Olsen, *The Importance and Value of Older Employees*, https://doi.org/10.1007/978-981-16-2861-0_5

younger colleagues?" In the presentation of findings, we have therefore chosen to present the findings in terms of long careers and high age, in addition to some everyday terms used by the interviewees.

5.1 Long Careers

Long careers are more than simply elapsed time and we would expect to find that older workers have been using theoretical knowledge from their professional education, whether as a nurse, a medical doctor, an engineer, an inspector, a cleaner or many other professions represented in these case studies. In addition they have acquired experience through many years of practice. The theoretical knowledge is important, but not sufficient. As one said:

> *... the theoretical knowledge can be always acquired. Without getting hands-on experience, you are pretty helpless really, the time you stand there and have to do something that you have never done before, but only have read about.*

Several described what they had learned through long careers as their way from being "fresh" in a field to having internalised knowledge to the point of being almost unconscious of knowing it. They talk about having performed job operations so many times that they do not have consciously to think about how to do it. Several people mentioned the ability to know-how, to carry out work operations without referring to the text book, whereas less experienced colleagues needed to follow the step-by-step instructions learned at school. Experience is not only about doing your own job, but also the ability to see the connection between your contribution and the contributions of others in the workplace. An older nurse explained:

> *The "fresh ones" mostly see their own job. The patient doesn't come in for general anesthesia. The experienced see the connection [between different elements of the treatment], the team [needed to treat the patient].*

This kind of expertise can help in performance of your job:

> *But when you ask what's the difference between someone with 10 years of experience and one with 30 years of experience, I think one difference is that (...) with 30 years or 40 years of experience, you don't need so much time to*

prepare for things. I'm not saying there are no drawbacks to that, but there are some advantages to being able to go into different situations, and quite complex situations and, without requiring all the world's preparation because we have some experience to rely on. (...) So we have some such well-used tools that we know work and that we can at least use to buy ourselves time to figure out what to do next. And it's one of those skills that might be a little "silent", or it's hard to describe. Pretty hard to develop, but it comes with age, with age and experience.

The Expert (as defined by Dreyfus & Dreyfus, 1986) has moved beyond proficiency and developed learning at a level where it has become part of their body, their being. They intuitively know-how to perform an operation, and can do so without thinking about why and how they do it this or that way.

As one older worker described it:

Those things that are buried deep down in the memory, and so when being asked a question, it just pops up. Then you have an answer to just that question.

This description reminds us of what Dreyfus and Dreyfus (1986) calls intuition and define as the result of deep situational involvement in similar situations. Intuition is expressed through an understanding that "performs effortlessly in seeing similarities to earlier experiences" (Dreyfus & Dreyfus in Hammarén, 2006: 210). When our informant talks about "things that are buried deep in the back of their heads" and being actualised or reactivated when in a similar situation, this is precisely the experience-based, internalised competence that "comes to life", is recalled and used. As someone described it:

It is difficult, because such knowledge has been so integrated in who you are, so it's difficult to identify it and talk about it.

Long careers, based on many years of work experience, enable employees to develop an ability to recognise situations and know-how to act upon them. Nurses talked about the "*clinical eye*", the ability to recognise minor symptoms as indicators of an underlying condition. Long experience lets them recognise connections between seemingly unrelated factors and know-how to act on this knowledge.

Inspectors from the Inspectorate also talked about the ability to recognise small details that might indicate bigger problems worth pursuing during the inspection. As one said: "Disorder in the reception area might indicate disorder in more important areas". Occupational Safety and Health (OSH) is about systematic work to eliminate safety hazards, and if safety is breached in one area it might be in others. One talked about noticing electric plugs, plugged into other plugs, laying in heaps on the floor in the reception area. This was an indicator that made her be extra observant about safety procedures and practice in other, more important areas of the enterprise.

They also talked about relational factors, and one mentioned the importance of how management and union representatives talked during meetings with inspectors. Did the union representative listen attentively to what the managers said or did they look down? Who did most of the talking? Such things could indicate areas worth pursuing in separate talks afterwards.

Long work experience includes having been through a lot of different situations, which can be an advantage:

> *And one thing that I'm thinking about, it's that it takes a great deal more to surprise me. I mean, we've been in quite a few different situations and constellations... It takes a lot more before we get taken by surprise or something that comes as a surprise.*

Long careers can also be useful in more specific situations. For example, one older surgeon talked about types of medical operations that had gone out of practice, but might still be needed in rare situations. As younger doctors were unfamiliar with these operations, the "old skills" of older doctors became valuable and important again.

> *Same with, for example, having split the main artery, such as aortic aneurysm. Before then, they had open surgery. Then these stents came in, which radiologists insert via the groin and which expand and keep the arteries open (…). And that leads to the fact that there is no one who operates aortic aneurysm anymore. (...) Those who operate, they get so little training because everything is done by the radiologists, so when someone comes in whom radiologists can't treat, the expertise for surgical treatment of aortic aneurysm is perhaps worse now than it was 10-15 years ago, when everyone was operated. There is something about the profession that makes it valuable sometimes to*

have a historical understanding and have been involved and done things for many years.

We also found examples where older employees mastered multiple forms of carrying the same surgical operations. Their "old skills" provided them with an alternative to the method learned by younger colleagues. This made it possible for the older employees to choose the best method in certain situations came back into use, something which they regarded as an advantage.

In the orthopedics, for the past 10 years there has been a trend of using tendons from the back of the thigh, hamstring tendons to make a new cruciate ligament, and operate that way. We used to take a piece of bone here, then we took a bit of the tendon that goes here between the kneecap and the calf also we took a bone bit where we also made a new cruciate ligament of it. It also turned out that taking tendons from behind the thigh is just fine, but for active people - and these are often active young people - then it stretches over time and then it becomes slacker again and there is a chance that it will go again. Whereas if you take the patellar tendon, and you need to make some special arrangements to attach it to the bone. While this one is stronger and holds better for... for active young people. But now there are few surgeons in Norway and none in Sweden who can actully do this patellar tendon type of operation. So they have to start training again, because they can only operate using the hamstring tendons.

Long careers are not only useful in the two organisations we mainly draw on in this analysis. We have asked similar questions in another public organisation, and found similar examples. One interviewee had worked for many years leading projects. Many of these projects were related to ICT systems used by the Norwegian state, but although they all had ICT in common they had different aims, different participating partners and vastly different budgets and timeframes. When thinking about what he had learned throughout his career, he said that there were lots of small details that he picked up from the different projects, like how to write good contracts, how to resolve conflicts between participants in a diplomatic way. The most valuable projects for his own learning had been the one which were most controversial and for which he had received most criticism. Although the project was a success, in the end, many of the incidents in the project were reported in the media and criticised. The interviewee still thinks about how he dealt with this particular project every time he plans a new project or helps a younger colleague to plan.

Apart from dealing with conflicts and with the media, another thing he learned gradually, was to expect and not be afraid of the enormous complexity of most of the projects. “When I read a project proposal, I know that it is like an iceberg, the person writing the proposal is probably only aware of 10% of what needs to be done and what can go wrong in the project”. “I know that we have to go deeper into the material, the aims, the questions, the expectations before we can make a realistic plan”. He told us he did not have a list or some kind of recipe for success in the early stages of planning and approving new projects, he described what he knew as “gut feeling, but a gut feeling you develop over time, you just know when to dive in and investigate more and when to let it go”. He also mentioned the importance of seeing the project proposal from multiple viewpoints, the societal benefits as well as the financial outlay and risk. He also described how he considered the motives of the different people involved in writing initial proposals and whether they were political, organisational, social, etc., and how important this could be later especially if something unexpected happened. The interviewee also mentioned that some colleagues saw him as a bit of a nuisance because he always wanted more information, wanted to analyse more risks, but he was encouraged to see that some younger colleagues were beginning to copy his critical questioning before they accepted project proposals.

The theme of multiple viewpoints mentioned in the last example was echoed by another interviewee who talked about how his understanding of subtleties had developed over time. An important part of his job was communication and he described how one never really learns enough about the different ways what one says and does can be interpreted and understood by different recipients. He explained that he was highly educated and had attended many courses on communication and felt he was fairly up to date with regard to both theory and techniques, however he described examples of how he could help a manager to make a project implementation a success or failure by adjusting their word, their voice, attitude and body language. Often he could not explain it to the manager, he had to show them, so that the managers could copy him.

> *I don't know if I have gained any insight into this, I think it is more like a good hypothesis which I take with me that some solutions are better than others.*

An interviewee took up a theme popular with management, standardisation of routines and support systems. He described how managers had announced that their department was going to implement "best practice" in all their administrative routines.

> *Best practice is all very well and there are lots of advantages, but once the train is rolling people stop considering the consequences. It just becomes an exercise where you cross off how many routines are now standardised. I know that our department can benefit from standardising some routines, but not everything. There are some tasks that we carry out, which are particular to us and the routines have developed gradually over time. I would say that we already have best practice for us on these routines. If we standardise and do these tasks in the same way as all other state departments, we will be reducing the quality of our work.*

The example the employee was unhappy with, was related to new routines for archiving documents and use of standard document templates. After considering this for a while he decided to take issue with the new routines and make a case for some exceptions in his department. He said he knew that his boss would need good arguments to gain approval so he and some colleagues spent some of their spare time building a case. The employee concluded that he would never have dared to contest a management decision in this way if he had not had the respect of colleagues and management, which he maintained had been developed slowly over the years.

5.1.1 Long Careers and Age Diversity

Experience-based knowledge often needs to be "unpacked", explicated. By working with younger colleagues the older workers are being asked questions that force them to articulate this expert knowledge and reflect on their own internalised practice. Also several people, both in the hospital and the Inspectorate, talked about the advantages younger workers bring, to set off the experience-based knowledge of the older workers.

Mostly they pointed to the digital competence of younger workers. Several of the older workers talked about a digital divide between younger colleagues and themselves. Younger colleagues who had "grown up" with digital technology were perceived as much more comfortable and competent using digital tools. Some said that this was an advantage of age diversity, because then they could help each other. Some talked about the net generation, echoing Tapscott (1998, 2009) who makes a divide between those growing up with digital technology and those being introduced to it as adults. Even if not all younger workers were familiar with the digital tools, they were seen as much more comfortable using it and happy to try out new functions and find new ways of using it in their local context.

Younger colleagues were also described as more eager in other fields, as in their energy and willingness to learn new things.

He has all the energy, the willingness to dig down and find out things.

The presence of age diversity provides the potential for sharing of knowledge and experiences and may prompt the older workers to explicate their tacit knowledge. Some interviewees told us that when younger colleagues asked questions and wanted explanations, the older employees needed to reflect on why they act in certain way, in order to be able to explain it to others. The experienced older workers can also serve as help and security for less experienced colleagues. One informant talked about when she was younger and new in her job at the hospital, how much more secure she felt when she worked with colleagues with long experience. She worked as a bioengineer, taking samples from patients and analysing them. Wrong results could be fatal, and she worked in shifts where they were only two people at the same time. Being with someone who was experienced in the job added to her feeling of security, so when she needed to consult she appreciated the older, more experienced colleague. A working environment consisting of both older and younger employees has the potential to develop complementarity, where both older and younger employees benefit from each other's knowledge, as her example demonstrates.

Mentoring or shoulder-to-shoulder learning are ways to combine mentors with long experience with younger colleagues, eager to learn. Both the hospital and Inspectorate had such systems although the practice was somewhat influenced by practical and economic constraints. One suggestion to remedy these constraints was put forward by one informant. The workplace could recruit replacements for older workers about to retire 6 months before actual retirement. This way the experienced worker could spend that time training the replacement and ensuring the transfer of some experience. This would be an ideal solution, but a more common situation was where "he got some speeches and flowers and then he was gone". It was pointed out that this suggestion came with a price, but could both cut costs of training new recruits and serve to value the competence of the older workers. Several of the older workers we talked to were concerned about who was to replace them and their knowledge when they retired. They also talked about the paradox of feeling valued while they were employed, but seeing the same knowledge, which made them valuable, was not being transferred and therefore lost as soon as they retired. As someone said:

> *If what I know is so valuable, why am I not given opportunities to share that knowledge while I am still here?*

Many older workers work flat out till the day they retire and the transfer is up to the individuals involved. Initiatives and measures to promote active ageing at the workplace level, could be aimed at remedying this situation.

5.1.2 Long Careers in the Same Job—Seniority in the Workplace

Some interviewees viewed seniority, or length of service in the same organisation, as an advantage, as they know-how things have developed into today's practice. Several of our informants also mentioned the usefulness of knowing people in different parts of the organisation. Who to go to if you have a problem or question even if it is not in your department.

There were several examples of how long service or seniority could be an advantage. You know-who to talk to, because you have been there a long time. You know there have been cases like the recent ones you are facing, so you know where to look for documentation of how it was handled last time. Someone talked about rare cases, being rare because they happened rarely, and "Norway being a small country so some cases only come along every few years".

Knowing how the workplace has developed was considered an advantage, as one knows why things are the way they are now and what kind of process has gone before to make it so. Older inspectors talked about the advantage of knowing how today's practice has developed and what kind of political and practical processes lie behind it. Both legislation and practice has changed over the years. Knowing why these changes have come about and what arguments are behind the changes, makes it easier to both understand and communicate the meaning of the law and today's regulatory practice.

Some of the experienced older inspectors in the Inspectorate also pointed to the value of still having saved physical reports from previous campaigns that had not been digitalized due to expired laws or regulations. Some of those who had worked in the Inspectorate for many years often had their own paper archives and pointed to still relevant (and useful) descriptions of physical and chemical risk factors although the legislation might have changed.

Some forms of practical knowledge can only be developed after many years at the same workplace. A janitor at a health institution told us he had been asked to work beyond retirement age. The buildings were undergoing reconstruction and it turned they lacked plans of underground pipes and cables. The janitor had been there for many years and knew where they could safely dig based on previous experience. One can only hope they drew up plans while he was still around to assist!

5.1.3 *Long Careers in Different Jobs*

Long worklife experience may not only be in the same place to be of value. In the Inspectorate long careers in different jobs were also described as an advantage, as it gives a comprehensive knowledge about working life that is useful for inspectors in their supervision of a wide range of Norwegian enterprises. Norway has several national Inspectorates supervising different fields from safety in the oil sector to the agricultural sector. One older worker talked about her previous experience from one of these different fields:

> *I know what it is to be out on supervision. To be able to find the balance between control and guidance.*

The informants at the hospital also recounted examples demonstrating the value of having worked in other places in the past. As the people we talked to were mainly health personnel, they talked about jobs in other parts of the health sector, as in doctors' surgeries, nursing homes or similar. Knowing how the health sector in Norway is organised, what the relationships between state owned or municipal services are, turned out to be very useful when meeting patients who were referred from or to other parts of the health services. What they have experienced of services before being admitted to hospital and what can they expect after being released? Knowledge of such questions could be used to reassure patients. We were told of being asked questions about home care, about who will do the follow up after a hospital treatment, about what is important to consider when back at home again, as examples where it helped to know-how home care was organised and what to expect from it. Although not directly related to the disease or injury for which the patient was hospitalised, remembering to ask questions about nutrition and physical activity was also one example mentioned. "Old, frail and living alone" can often be an indicator of under-stimulation and even malnutrition. Experienced nurses talked to their patients about such things and asked about how they had been living before the hospitalisation and about how they could seek help in such areas when returning home again.

Examples from the state department stress the same points. One interviewee was working on a temporary project, which was not within her area of expertise. The interviewee was educated in languages and had studied and worked abroad before taking up a position in a government service organisation. As her career developed she moved from a health-related part of the public sector, to agriculture, history and culture, then on to a more administrative department. She had been a manager with responsibility for large budgets and many employees, before she was asked to lead a project which would be very visible and have high public interest. She was originally asked to work on the project for 3 years, but at the time of interview, she had been working on it for 9 years. Although the project was considered very successful, she actually wanted to do something else with her last few years before retiral, but she was generally considered irreplaceable. What made her so irreplaceable, we asked? She began to describe how she used what she had learned about manoeuvring through the state system in different situations. She had used her network which crossed many organisational boundaries and had always managed to get help and support from previous colleagues.

Like another government employee who mentioned the nuances of communication, she also mentioned this and how long it took to understand. She explained how she had helped lawyers to rewrite information in such a way that it could be understood by the public. She described how she had learned to discuss with experts from different fields while she worked with history and culture.

> *… when you are out there at a site talking to an expert, you just have to try different ways of talking and find out what works. Experts are experts, whatever their field. You have to talk to them in the right way. You have to trust them and respect their knowledge, but you have to be brave and ask them to explain things in a simple way. I think I learned this a long time ago, but I've never put it into words until now. It's is really important to know this and I would never be able to do my job without this skill, or maybe it's knowledge, I'm not sure. I think it's just a way of doing things.*

As well as communication, this interviewee mentioned how she had become reflective in recent years.

> *I used to rush at things before, I thought everyone was watching me, but now I reflect over the task in-hand. I think a lot about the different places I worked, here we did this and here we did that, here we followed these rules. Then I think what do we do now, what does the department need, what does the public need. Then I go and get the people and resources I need. I try to motivate and inspire the people I need and make sure all the formalities are in place.*

This interviewee had quite a lot of freedom in her job and because of her varied past, she often received invitations to conferences in different fields of expertise. She said how she sometimes chose to attend conferences in different fields because it might give her a new understanding or a different perspective. She was of the opinion that her varied career had helped her and made her the perfect match, or the irreplaceable employee, for her current position.

5.2 Age

Beyond the many models of competence, old age might play a separate role in their ability to perform in their jobs. Several examples of age as authority was mentioned. A nurse working with small children with severe eczema talked about meeting a crying child and a nervous, young mother and being able to calm them down. The nurse saying "Relax, we'll manage this" was believed because she had the authority of age, of having seen the same situation many, many times before.

Age as authority can be an advantage when dealing with patients. Some patients can be demanding or difficult, and an older nurse can be better at handling such situations. As one described it:

You don't get intimidated by difficult patients.

Not only patients can be difficult. Also colleagues at higher levels in the organisation can be a challenge:

You become more confident in yourself, you know what you stand for and it has not always been easy being a cleaner in this place. Because there's a hierarchy here. And we're regrettably at the bottom, which I haven't quite... I don't accept that and I'll let them know when they're stomping all over me.

An older nurse described age and long experience as an advantage when facing arrogant behavior from doctors:

I was here when you were only an intern.

Age can give you both "charisma and clout". Older workers can give the impression that they know what they are doing because of long experience, and are listened to where a younger worker might be mistrusted or come across as less convincing.

My job consists very much of representing the manager in organisational processes where we are going to plan or we are going to change. (...) And they are strong people, strong people, who are leaders, (...). The fact that they are strong also means that there are very strong wills (...), so there have been fights and you feel that it helps to have experience with that type of processes. A mixture of being listening, but also knowing when you need to put your foot down; now we have to decide something. So it's experience. Now, there aren't very many young people in this job, but someone who comes with less experience, they get challenged and are in for a hard time.

Similarly, in the Inspectorate case, the older inspectors talked about the authority of age as an advantage when confronting managers and enterprises that did not comply with laws and regulations. In one example they described how they closed down a work site, and how this was made easier because they looked so obviously experienced, and their authority was respected and they were listened to.

I realise that when I tell them I've been in this job for 24-25 years, and I have been doing this and that, people straighten their backs a little bit, they listen more. (...) Age is obviously authority. But of course you have to behave and know what you're talking about whatever age.

Age as authority was also mentioned in the state department interviews. When asked if age was an advantage at work, one interviewee described how she found it easier to make herself heard and how it felt easier to speak directly and put career ambitions and personal aims aside. As she said:

I don't think I could talk in capital letters when I was younger. Now I can say it as it is. I feel more comfortable and safe saying what I really think is right. I know it is based on what I have done before and I know that people look at me a see someone who knows what she is talking about. By nature I am really quite a shy and careful person, but now it easier to demand things, to insist on things which I know are important. I think it is much easier to make my voice heard now, that it was 30 years ago. That is the way I feel and I don't have to think about my career anymore and I don't have any personal motives anymore, I just think about doing the best I can.

A colleague was more daring and said how she did not actually follow the standard ways of working when she knew they would just cause problems in the future.

They will find out eventually that some of the new routines were wrong, but I can't wait for that. They can hang me as a rebel if they want, I don't care.

Daring to speak, was something which came up in several interviews and was considered quite important by most interviewees. The examples given were often related to policy or policy aims or to directives from government ministries. It was considered important that civil servants should be able to stand up or speak out when necessary and not be nervous or intimidated by the political standing or the authority of others. Several stated that they not been aware of this when they were younger, or that they had not been willing to speak out about risks or alternative ways of doing things.

Another employee was less certain about the benefits of age, but described some of the differences. She described how annoyed she was at a new ICT system which had been implemented, but she did not want to be viewed as "a grumpy old woman who doesn't like technology, or who doesn't want to learn anything new". However, this interviewee did find a way of working with the new system. She discussed it with colleagues and via a process of sharing their experiences of trial and error, they agreed on a way of working which suited them and fitted in with the ICT system.

One interviewee described the difference as being a change in loyalties, he reflected that when he was younger his loyalties lay with his department or perhaps at times with himself as he tried to carve out a career. Now he maintained that his loyalties were to his field of expertise, or to his profession and he thought this made him a much better employee than he had been when he was younger.

5.2.1 *Age and Life Phase*

We can also view age as an indicator of where you are in life. Different life phases have different focus and challenges.

> *When you are older, you have more space in your life, not so many demands on your time. I can watch football training or watch my grandchildren playing, but it's not my responsibility to get them ready, so life is different when you don't have care for your own young children.*

Not having the double burden of full job and small children at home allowed them more time to commit to their careers. They also talked about having more time for restitution after a busy day at work, if needed. Some talked about having more time to keep fit, as they didn't have to hurry home from work to look after their children.

At the same time, there were some who pointed out that caring for children is starting to be replaced by caring for older parents. With increased life expectancy, the employed 60-year-old today may still have parents in their 80s or 90s, so the burden of care can return in a new form. Ennals and Hilsen (2011) describe older workers as "the jam in the intergenerational sandwich", combining responsibility for grown children with care for elderly and infirm relations. In addition to informal care of elderly relatives, "middle-aged carers, on the other hand, might simultaneously be shouldering the responsibility to care for their own (grand)-children" (Hoffmann & Rodrigues, 2010: 10). This defines them as the sandwich generation or the pivot generation (Mooney et al., 2002), or "the jam in the intergenerational sandwich" (Ennals & Hilsen, 2011: 245). In this way some of the older workers may never really leave care obligations towards family members. Still caring for older relations is different and less demanding than caring for small children, as the Norwegian welfare state has (fairly) good access to professional care. Although caring for older relations might be felt as stressful, as some of the hospital workers reported, Norwegian studies (Gautun & Hagen, 2010; Midtsundstad, 2009) have found that caring obligations have little effect on retirement patterns, and therefore we can assume that many older workers are still working and might be in this situation.

More time to themselves or changed demands on their time can be a result of the phase of life they are in. There are also other effects of age and life phase. For example, many of the older workers talked about how the experience in earlier phases made them more tolerant of younger colleagues who were struggling. They talked about having been through tough times before and one said: “I’m more tolerant as a grandmother than I was as a mother”. Mature older workers can be a great support for their younger colleagues, but also for the people they encounter as part of their jobs.

5.2.2 *Age and the Body*

Age also changes our physical perceptions of ourselves as well as other people’s perceptions of us. This can have down-sides, but as one older worker pointed out, it may also be liberating:

> *And at work, well, I think maybe most of us are fighting the battle that we know we lose, about physical appearance. Isn’t that right? We know it’s always a process, a process of grief, right? But then there’s something in it that’s kind of a relief and that, relax, it’s not that important now. A lot of people say they think they’re better off after they don’t have to think of themselves as potential sex objects.*

If this self-acceptance and relief from sexual roles make interacting with colleagues or patients easier and less stressful, age can have advantages in everyday life. Most Norwegian hospital workers are female, so this might be a gendered experience. One woman who worked with counselling talked about age as changing her relationship to men she counselled. When she was younger, her relationship with young male patients had been more difficult. They “needed to show off their masculinity”, as she described it. As she grew older, her role changed from competitor to nurturer, which made the relationship easier:

And the young men, - I've no chance there. I'll be a mom to them. I think they think that's all right.

The relationships between men and women are gendered, and age seems to change the role of women at the workplace. Older women have access to other, "safer" roles, such as mother (or grandmother) towards their colleagues, patients and others.

5.2.3 Age and Generation

Age is also about being of a certain age in relation to others. Being of the same age as the people one interacts with at work can mean having been through the same period of time, sharing cultural, historical and political references. Matching age with the patients might make the relationship easier, whether it is about sharing musical references, knowing the same stories or having watched the same historical events.

Older workers at the hospital told stories about working with patients with dementia and being able to engage them by referring to events from their youth. Until 1991 Norway only had one TV channel (except areas close to the Swedish border that could also watch Swedish television), and older patients had grown up with one choice of TV programmes only. One nurse told a story of a patient with dementia making references to a children's programme on TV, and because she also had grown up with those programmes she could recognise the reference and actually managed to engage the patient in a discussion about that programme. "Same-age references" can be useful when interacting with others.

Also inspectors in the Inspectorate talked about having been having a better understanding of the challenges faced by enterprises because they had been through the same things. One inspector talked about digital competence (or lack thereof) when meeting companies that struggled to use online information and services. Where younger colleagues would take digital competence for granted, the older inspectors could easily understand and sympathise with struggling managers.

Same-age references and experiences are an aspect of age, but it is also something quite specific. We may call it generational knowledge or same-age knowledge. As such it is not restricted to older workers, but encompasses all same-age groups. Still, our older workers used this same-age knowledge to their benefit when working with people of the same age. In this way it can also be seen as part of late career competence.

5.3 Willingness and Opportunity to Learn

The interviews provided many examples where interviewees, unprompted, described their learning experiences. Highly qualified workers were taking master's degrees in management at the age of 55 and over, while others were learning new languages in their free time. There was a high level of awareness of the value of knowledge and the importance of continually developing it. As one interviewee said:

You cannot just lean back and assume that what you know today will be just as valuable and useful tomorrow.

Most of the employees were positive to learning new things and some even seemed surprised that anyone should think otherwise. Willingness to learn new things and reflect on existing practices was very much present in the material. If learning is to happen, we must assume a willingness to learn, to expose oneself to situations outside the familiar, but also the presence of opportunities to learn new things. From the interviews it seems like these opportunities were often present in their everyday work.

I learn something new every day.

There are always new challenges which I can learn from.

New learning is not only connected to their everyday work, but also from working with others:

I look forward to working with my colleagues every day, they are so experienced and I can learn so much from them.

Such answers may be a result of the types of work our informants have. Both hospital workers and inspectors meet new people and new challenges on a fairly regular basis.

The job is so varied, you never know what new issues will arise, but I learn from all of them.

Many jobs may be more static and with more monotonous tasks, where the opportunity for new learning is smaller. In our cases many of the jobs described offered opportunities to learn new things.

It is not only the desire and ability to identify opportunities for learning which was obvious in our cases, but also their willingness to share their knowledge with others.

> *I look forward to contributing to change and developing new ways of working.*

Several mentioned that they viewed it as an important responsibility, while another recounted an example where a younger colleague had asked her how to do something, the interviewee could not explain and offered to take notes the next time she did the task herself and explain to the junior afterwards. The latter is of course an example of tacit knowledge, which is notoriously difficult to identify and to share. In this example the willingness of the senior to spend time on cooperating with the junior made this possible.

These are of course only examples, but they paint a picture of workers who accept novelty and change and for whom learning is viewed as continuous activity integrated with their everyday work.

5.4 Summary of Findings

We asked the older workers about what they considered the advantages or usefulness of long work careers and high age. In their own words they talked about situations where long experience allowed them to act quickly and correctly, where their experience-based expertise helped them perform their job tasks well and where this competence was also an advantage for their less experienced colleagues and for the workplace. They talked about knowing *why* they did what they did in the ways they did it. They also mentioned the advantage to them of having been around long enough to know-*who* to ask if they needed help.

They gave us examples of situations where long experience, both in worklife and in the same workplace was useful. Long worklife careers are related to age, and they talked about the advantages of having lived long and been through life's ups and downs. Age gave the authority and made them feel secure in performance of their work. Being older also allowed them references and experiences they could share with same-age users of their services. As older they also found themselves in a life phase with less care obligations for small children, and some talked about getting older as entering different roles with different expectations than when they were younger. In our discussion of their experiences and stories we basically sorted the material according to the broad categories from the interview guide (experience and age) and used broad everyday terms as they introduced them.

In the next chapter we will move away from the terms used by the interviewees themselves and discuss the data from different analytical perspectives, where we will draw on theory to better explore and understand late career competence in the workplace.

Reference

Dreyfus, H. L., & Dreyfus, S. E. (1986). *Mind over machine: The power of human intuition and expertise in the era of the computer*. Free Press: University of Michigan.

CHAPTER 6

Discussion/What Do These Findings Tell Us

Abstract In this chapter we present the empirical data and organise them in such a way that can be used to improve our understanding of what over 50s have learned at work, what skills they have developed and how they have found their age and experience to be an advantage in carrying out their working tasks.

Keywords Competence · Experience · Learning

6.1 Introduction to Discussion

Here we analyse the findings and group them in such a way that can be used to improve our understanding of what over 50s have learned at work, what skills they have developed and how they have found their age and experience to be an advantage in carrying out their working tasks. In this way we hope to develop a basis upon which we can discuss the concept of senior competence. The categories which have emerged from our analysis of the data are communication, confidence, understanding of context, and a group of abilities which we have classified as variety, such as variety of workplaces, tasks, colleagues and methods or ways of doing things. We have also identified a category which we have called seeing the big picture and lastly, we include a more general category which we have called maturity. These categories may not cover all our findings and are

A. I. Hilsen and D. S. Olsen, *The Importance and Value of Older Employees*, https://doi.org/10.1007/978-981-16-2861-0_6

probably not an exhaustive description of what seniors know, however the categories provide us with a variety of lenses through which we can view our findings and reflect upon what the data tells us in order to make sense of it. Many of the cases illustrate more than one category, and we have chosen the examples discussed in this chapter based on the lens through which we are viewing it.

6.2 Communication

The interviewees were not asked directly about communication, or how they had learned to communicate, but in the course of the interviews we observed several examples of situations where they demonstrated clear abilities to use language, tone, choice of words and body language to communicate. For example, several interviewees explained how challenging it was to explain the complexity of new regulations before they were operationalised. There was one example of an employee in a government department who had considered this was conscious of her own abilities as an experienced communicator. As she said:

> … *when you are out there at a site talking to an expert, you just have to try different ways of talking and find out what works. Experts are experts, whatever their field. You have to talk to them in the right way.*

This suggests an awareness of what is the right way of communicating.

One interviewee described how her experience working with lawyers had made her aware of the different ways in which one can talk about the same themes. She became more aware of this difference when she worked on historical and cultural issues. The different groups of employees communicated in different ways and stressed different things and presented information to others in different formats and used different words. Again, a clear awareness, not only of the importance of communication, but also how communication can be used to work with different groups. The latter example is interesting because the interviewee linked her current understanding to her own varied career path and to her own development over time.

These reflections suggest that this experienced employee had developed a kind of translator ability, whereby she considers the receiver of the information first, then decides how she will present the information.

Some of the other examples suggest that something similar is happening, although employees may not be aware of what they are doing, such as the nurse who knows exactly what to say and how to say it, in order to calm patients. This was not only an act of compassion, but also improved the efficiency of the task and made the job easier.

Sharing information with younger colleagues is also an important, but perhaps little recognised skill found among older employees. One of the examples from the hospital case illustrates this quite well, where an older employee remembered how her older colleague communicated a sense of security.

One of the government employees mentioned talking about communication to new recruits. The younger employees were used to communicating in sound bytes, i.e. short summarised pieces of digital information. The older employees, on the other hand, had spent years honing their skills at report writing. They claimed they could communicate complex information to multiple readers in an unambiguous way without causing offence to any group. They were ready and willing to share this information with their colleagues.

6.3 Confidence

"Confidence is a belief in oneself, the conviction that one has the ability to meet life's challenges and to succeed—and the willingness to act accordingly. Being confident requires a realistic sense of one's capabilities and feeling secure in that knowledge", according to Psychology Today (https://www.psychologytoday.com/intl/basics/confidence).

Our interviewees tell us about several factors that contribute to what we perceive as their feeling of confidence. They talk about being competent in their jobs, but also about being confident in life. They talk about being in a phase of life where they are more relaxed, more tolerant and accepting of others.

This confidence is not only of benefit in doing their jobs, but can also help and support younger colleagues. One informant talked about when she was younger and new in her job at the hospital, how much more secure she felt when she worked with colleagues with long experience. Being with someone who was experienced in the job added to her feeling of security, so when she needed to consult she appreciated the older, more experienced colleague.

Confidence, as described by our interviewees, is also based on feeling competent at a high level. Not only knowing how to do your job, but being able to act fast in a situation, whereas younger colleagues need to "do it by the book" and think about how to act. This very much reflects the learning process described by Dreyfus and Dreyfus (1986), where the learned moves through the steps from Novice, to Advanced Beginner, Competence, Proficiency and Expertise. According to Dreyfus and Dreyfus: "The beginning student wants to do a good job, but lacking any coherent sense of the overall task he judges his performance mainly by how well he follows learned rules. After he acquires more than just a few rules, the exercise of his skill requires so much concentration that his capacity to talk or listen to advice is severely limited. Like the training wheels on a child's first bicycle, these rules allow the accumulation of experience, but soon they must be put aside to proceed" (Dreyfus & Dreyfus, 1986: 22).

This is reflected in how our older workers talk about younger colleagues and their need to "go by the book". Over time they talk about older workers having developed to a stage where they know how to do things without having to refer to any specific manual or think about why and how to perform a job operation. They have become proficient at their jobs. As described by Dreyfus and Dreyfus: "As events modify the salient features, plans expectations, and even the relative salience of features will gradually change. No detached choice or deliberation occurs. It just happens, apparently because the proficient performer has experienced similar situations in the past and memories of them trigger plans similar to those that worked in the past and anticipations of events similar to those that occurred" (Dreyfus & Dreyfus, 1986: 28).

Our interviewees described situations where they "just knew how to act" without having to consciously think about it. They talked about having the competence and confidence to do their work, whether that was as nurse, cleaner or inspector, because they had age and experience. The example of the cleaner who felt secure enough in her job to not feel intimidated by doctors she had first met when they were interns, shows that confidence is also dependent on age and long work career. We were told the same story from the older inspectors who had the confidence to do their job, as they knew it should be done, in difficult situations.

In many ways we could say that the late career competence described by our interviewees seems to reflect a high degree of confidence in being able to cope at work and a sense of their job situation being comprehensible to them; they know what to do, how to do it and why it should be done in this way. They experience the demands of the job are manageable and they believe the job they do is meaningful. Coping at work is dependent of several factors, both personal/individual and contextual/environmental, where the environment includes physical surroundings as well as social demands/support (Daatland & Solem, 2011: 99). Coping is often seen as a personality trait, as exemplified by the concept of self-efficacy (Bandura, 1997) or sense of coherence (Antonovsky, 1985). Although such traits are often seen as fairly stable over the lifetime, both Bandura and Antonovsky accept that they can change over time. The concepts are dynamic, which indicates that they are open to change.

Antonovsky's sense of coherence (SOC) consists of three components: comprehensibility, manageability and meaningfulness. Does the individual perceive the situation one finds oneself as comprehensible, is it manageable and is it meaningful? The SOC is defined as: "The extent to which one has a pervasive, enduring though dynamic, feeling of confidence that one's environment is predictable and that things will work out as well as can reasonably be expected" (Antonovsky, 2002: 128; 2000: 37). Antonovsky developed his concept through studies of people who, in spite of having been through horrible ordeals, such as Holocaust survivors, maintained a feeling of positive health. A strong SOC is Antonovsky's answer to the question of what makes a person more likely to feel less stress and tension, and to believe that he or she can meet demands.

Late career competence as described by our interviewees reflects a high degree of confidence in being able to cope and meet the demands of their jobs. They also have the confidence to accept that they sometimes make mistakes. Based on experience and age, they know-how to do their jobs and can reflect on why they do it the way they do, and they talked about the need to be constantly learning through practice and reflection.

6.4 Understanding of Context

What is the context of this experience-based knowledge, this late career competence of older workers? The competence is connected to an understanding of context, as they all talk about their competence in a specific workplace context or setting, performing activities that are meaningful given the context of the type of work they do. The older workers in our cases talk about long experience has taught them how to do their job with expertise, they talk about carrying the history of the workplace, being tradition bearers, knowing how and why things were done differently in the past and even having practical knowledge (such as referring to physical features of the workplace) acquired having worked in the same workplace for many years. They are tuned in to the local environment and know who to go to if they have questions (know-who). They not only see their own place and contribution in the workplace but they also demonstrate awareness of colleagues' needs and abilities and talk about caring and sharing with their younger colleagues.

Context and setting are two related concepts, still we understand them as referring to separate phenomena. *Settings* refer to where something happens. As defined by the WHO (in the Ottawa Charter, 1986): "Health is created and lived by people within the settings of their everyday life; where they learn, work, play and love" (WHO, 1986: 3–4). The field of health promotion has adopted the settings approach, where things not only happen in a setting, but you could also strive to make the setting supportive of promoting health, the so-called settings approach of working with a setting (Schriven & Hodgins, 2012). Settings from this perspective is where your life is lived, in a fairly physical/spatial meaning. We talk about worklife, or even more specific the workplace, as settings where our older workers perform their work. Late career competence is played out in the workplace settings specific to the jobs they have.

Context is a more complex phenomenon. Context can refer to the physical surroundings, but not in a purely objective sense. According to Bateson (1972: 186), *contexts*, and his connected concept of *frames*, are psychological concepts. They are concepts by which we organise and understand phenomena. Contexts can be used to describe fields of learning, as Guile (2006) talks about learning across the contexts of vocational curricula and workplace practice. His agenda is to conceptually bridge the gap between theory and practice in vocational/professional education, in order to develop an understanding of learning across the different contexts. Theories on learning tend to use context in many, and sometimes conflicting, ways (Dohn et al., 2018). Do we learn *in* a context or is the context the theoretical framework for understanding learning, as the examples of historical, cultural, social or national contexts for learning (ibid.: 1–2).

When we explore late career competence in the workplace as having given the older workers an understanding of context, we intentionally use the concept in both an empirical and theoretical sense. In an empirical sense, they understand and describe their competence, as competent practice in the performance of their work, with practical examples of situations and performances. In a theoretical sense, more in line with Bateson's understanding of context as a psychological concept (Bateson, 1972), they describe their competence as an understanding of their role and relationship to co-workers. As older workers they not only understand their own job and what it takes, but they talk about being aware of colleagues' needs and abilities. From this understanding also comes their examples of caring and sharing with their younger colleagues. Age not only gives experience; it also gives maturity. As one interviewee explained: "I'm more tolerant as a grandmother than I was as a mother". The ability to care for co-workers can be understood as a reflection of their understanding of context, not only in a practical, physical way, but also as a relationship with mutual dependence.

6.5 Variety

The longer the working career, the more we would expect the employee to have experienced. Over time many of them experience more of the same, while others amass a variety of different experiences. We found this idea of variety an interesting aspect of the long working career and chose to look more closely at how our interviewees experienced this and how it was useful for them.

One form of variety we identified, was having worked for different employers or having worked at different locations for the same employer. We would expect that this kind of mobility would have exposed employees to different forms of management, different challenges and different ways of dealing with these challenges. We would also expect that the employee would have met more people and perhaps have a larger network of contacts, than an employee who had remained at the same place throughout his or her career.

In one interview the "irreplaceable" project manager said that she had learned to "manoeuvre through the state system in different situations" always knew who to ask for help. Her network extended across several government departments where she had previously worked and included people with a wide variety of expertise. She actively maintained this network and even attended conferences outside her own area of expertise, with the aim of keeping herself up-to-date on what was happening in other areas, knowing who knew what and might be able to help her in the future. She had not really considered this to be a particular advantage until we interviewed her, it had just been the way she was used to working. Looking back on her she said she could see that it had been an advantage and made it easier for her to take chances, like daring to lead a project on new technology, daring to apply for a new position she was not sure she was qualified for.

Another example was a project manager who had worked on many different projects. He had worked within the public and the private sector and worked in several different departments in the public sector. He described how he always took what he had learned in earlier projects with him into new projects. When asked about the advantages this gave him, he described how he viewed new projects as icebergs, i.e. the largest part was hidden. He knew, almost instinctively, what questions to ask and where to dig for information and find potential weaknesses.

Another form of variety which emerged from interviews was variety in working tasks. This kind of variety was something which can affect those who remain in the same position and at the same location throughout their working career, but also those who move from one function to another. There are examples in the interview material of employees whose experience has made it possible for them to do the same task in different ways, or to experience doing a task with and without technology. Some of the benefits of varied ways of working were quite subtle, such as having multiple choices to consider when taking a decision or solving a problem. As one interviewee said, he no longer takes the first potential solution, he looks for the best.

An example of this can be seen in the interviewees who did not want to go on courses to learn new ICT systems, instead they chose to learn by trial and error or by asking colleagues. These employees were aware of the course they could have attended and there were no particular obstacles to their participating in organised training courses. They had, however, experienced new ICT systems before. They had also experienced doing the job manually, with little ICT support. This broad experience of different ways of working with technology and different ways of learning about technology provided them with choices. The advantage they mentioned was that they did not need to waste time on a 3-day course, what they learned was what they needed in order to do their work, not lots of other unnecessary technological functions.

We have also mentioned the example of a surgeon who was familiar with the traditional way of operating on an aortic aneurism as well as the more modern and simpler treatment of inserting stents. Younger colleagues were not educated in the traditional method and therefore it was not natural for them to recommend it or even to see it as an option for patients. The older surgeon however believed that his experience gave him more options in choosing the best treatment for his patient.

Another example of alternative ways of doing things can be seen in some of the examples where employees talked about a new standardised electronic archive system. They all understood the importance of classifying and storing government documents and had long experience of doing this and of finding (or not finding) documents. They did not contest the archiving system directly, what they reacted to, was the imposition of best practice. They considered that their long experience in the department had provided them with a wealth of experience and believed that their methods might in fact be the "best practice". Had they not had all this experience, they conceded that they would probably just have accepted the new system unaware that there were alternative ways of archiving.

6.6 Seeing the Big Picture

We have discussed how many experienced older employees can see alternative ways of doing things and have multiple interpretations of the same information, however we also found examples where relatedness and the ability to connect was considered valuable. One example was the nurse who talked about the "fresh ones" who were unable to see the relationship between all the different elements in the patient's treatment. For her, it was natural to see all these connections and she maintained that this made her work much more efficient, she could jump faster from one step to the next instead of plodding through all the basic steps.

In another example the inspectors checking on safety and security described how they began to form an opinion of the standards as soon as they entered the reception. In order to carry out a formal evaluation of a client, the inspectors must follow strict guidelines, but this example suggests that other criteria can influence the way in which the evaluation progresses. What the inspectors saw in the reception was not an alternative to what they found in the formal evaluation, but it was viewed as supplementary information which prepared them to look more carefully in the next phase. Their long experience told them that clients who received a critical evaluation of their security and safety often had a messy reception. They had identified a relationship between two situations, a relationship that turned up time and again. Noticing these small details and comparing them to past experiences was considered an advantage and the inspectors thought it made their evaluation more effective.

6.7 Maturity

In the interviews and discussions, we have heard many mentions of the *mature worker* and *maturity* as an aspect of being an experienced older worker. Maturation can be used to describe the process of reaching a stage of full or advanced development (Dictionary.com). Given such an understanding of maturity, it is obvious that mature workers have had years of experience and learning to facilitate the process of maturation.

Maturity also lends the individual authority in the sense of being listened to and having one's communications respected. Both the hospital workers and the inspectors talk about how age and experience have given them authority in their daily work. Whether it is the case of interacting with colleagues and patients in a hospital or with companies/organisations in their role as inspectors, the mature worker carries a combination of charisma and clout, of authority, when interacting with others. When describing the mature worker, several interviewees used the word "pondus". "Having pondus" in the sense of weight, importance, significance. The simple translation of pondus from latin is weight (physical), but it can also be used in transferred meaning. In addition, we find pondus used to mean important, significant, as in the sentences: "Cur tam magnum habet **pondus** "splendor veritatis"? (Why is the "splendour of truth" so **important**?), or "Anni iubilaris habita ratione, magnum **pondus** habere debebat Congressus Eucharisticus Internationalis". In the spirit of this Jubilee Year the International Eucharistic Congress was intended to have special **significance** (vatican.va at https://glosbe.com/la/en/pondus). In Norwegian the word pondus is widely used, both in its physical meaning (being big, heavy) and its transferred meaning as having clout, authority, being listened to and respected. Our mature workers acknowledge that age and experience have given them this authority, this pondus, and they experience situations where it has made their work easier.

Maturity describes the result of age and experience for the individual who has been open to learning and reflection throughout one's career. At the same time, the concept of maturity may hide the importance of the environment where this process has taken place. Maturity consists of more than age. When talking about mature wines or cheese, we don't just talk about old wine and cheese; we talk about refined products. Old wine can turn to vinegar and mouldy cheese is not an ideal unless you are a gorgonzola. They are refined as a result of the process they have been through. Stimulants have been added (bacterial cultures when it comes to cheese), storage facilities have been controlled and the process of maturation has been closely watched by the producers.

According to the Milk Quality Improvement Program at Cornell University (www.milkfacts.info): "There is a wide variety of bacterial cultures available that provide distinct flavor and textural characteristics to cheeses. (…) Even yeasts and molds are used in some cheeses to provide the characteristic colors and flavors of some cheese varieties. Torula yeast is used in the smear for the ripening of brick and limburger cheese. Examples of molds include Penicillium camemberti in camembert and brie, and Penicillium roqueforti in blue cheeses".

In a (fairly) similar manner mature workers are the result of a process where learning and experiences have been added over years, stimulants have been added as they received feedback from managers, colleagues and users, and they have developed in a work environment that not only hinders damage and disease, but provides a basis for a healthy and meaningful working situation.

6.7.1 What Have We Learned from This Analysis?

The interviews provided many examples where interviewees, unprompted, described their learning experiences. Highly qualified workers taking master's degrees in management at 55 and over, while others were learning new languages in their free time. There was a high level of awareness of the value of knowledge and the importance of continually developing it.

Some of the findings provide examples of what we define as the added advantages of age or maturity. Characteristics which can best be described as a mix of charisma and clout are attributed to the mature worker, the older worker. The older workers tell us about authority in situations where they are respected and listened to differently from younger colleagues. Where users of the services, such as patients or children might feel insecure, the mature worker can create a feeling of safety and provide emotional support in addition to their normal tasks.

Some characteristics were associated with age, such as what stage of life you are at, understanding society, values and attitudes that characterise the present generation of older workers, and age-specific references (being of the same age as the people with whom you interact and recognising the same stories or references). Older workers are in the latter part of their working career and might not be as ambitious and driven by the need to get promotion as younger workers might. Some talked about being more concerned by what they left behind when they retired than in "building a career". This was viewed as making them more generous in sharing knowledge and experience. Not only being a resource and support for their younger colleagues, but they could also be non-threatening to managers. One young manager said she relied on her oldest employees, as they were less interested in making careers for themselves and therefore more willing to share and support her when she asked.

The findings tell us of a wide array of advantages based on length of career and age. There are advantages for the older employee as well for their younger colleagues. Being competent in their jobs, having knowledge and experience to draw on and the maturity of age is an advantage for the older workers in performing their jobs, as described by several of our interviewees. It also makes these mature workers valuable as co-workers for younger and less experienced colleagues. In this way, there are also advantages for the enterprise as a whole. Mentoring, shadowing and mixed-age teams are all ways of using the complementary competence of younger and older workers to the advantage of the enterprise.

References

Antonovsky, A. (1985). *Health, stress, and coping*. San Francisco: Jossey-Bass Publishers.

Antonovsky, A. (2000). *Helbredets mysterium*. Hans Reitzels Forlag.

Antonovsky, A. (2002). Unravelling the mystery of health: How people manage stress and stay well. In D. F. Marks (Eds.), *The health psychology reader* (pp. 127–139). Sage.

Bandura, A. (1997). *Self-efficacy: The exercise of control*. W H Freeman/Times Books/Henry Holt & Co.

Bateson, G. (1972). *Steps to an ecology of mind*. Ballantine Books.

Daatland, S. O., & Solem, P. E. (2011). *Aldring og samfunn* (2nd ed.). Fagbokforlaget.

Dohn, N. B., Hansen, S. B., & Klausen, S. H. (2018). On the concept of context. *Edu. Sci, 8*, 111. https://doi.org/10.3390/edusci803111. www.mdpi.com/jpornal/education.

Dreyfus, H. L., & Dreyfus, S. E. (1986). *Mind over machine: The power of human intuition and expertise in the era of the computer*. Oxford: Basil Blackwell.

Guile, D. (2006). Learning across contexts. *Educational Philosophy and Theory, 38*(3), 251–268. https://doi.org/10.1111/j.1469-5812.2006.00193.x.

Schriven, A., & Hodgins, M. (2012). *Health promotion settings: Principles and practice*. Sage.

The Milk Quality Improvement Program, Cornell University, USA. Downloaded September 15th, 2020 from http://www.milkfacts.info/Milk%20Processing/Cheese%20Production.htm#CAge.

WHO (World Health Organization). (1986). *Ottawa Charter for Health Promotion*. WHO.

CHAPTER 7

The Wise Worker

Abstract In this chapter we consider the competence of older employees and how it has been developed and refined throughout their careers. We consider this competence in the light of earlier findings on the development of work-related knowledge and we suggest some new ways of interpreting the particular kind of competence older employees often have. We suggest that the concept of wisdom can be used to supplement our understanding of long career competence and based on our interview data we present a concept of the wise worker.

Keywords Wisdom · Experience · Age

The analysis of the findings in the previous chapter introduced some interesting issues, some of these are familiar, while others are perhaps less well defined. In this chapter we will attempt to improve these definitions and develop a concept. We begin by considering our findings in relation to the literature and earlier studies which we discussed in Chapters 2 and 3, and we summarise our understanding of the mature worker in terms of learning and competence. We then go a step further and attempt to supplement these descriptions by introducing the concept of the wise worker.

In Chapter 2 we presented some concepts of competence and knowledge at work. The findings from our interviews are interesting in relation

A. I. Hilsen and D. S. Olsen, *The Importance and Value of Older Employees*, https://doi.org/10.1007/978-981-16-2861-0_7

to earlier work on situated knowledge and professional knowledge and to a certain extent to the work on organisational knowledge. With regard to the latter, the questions we posed in interviews were more related to the individual and their colleagues, rather than the organisation. However, we did find examples which fit in well with Lundvall's model (1996). We found many examples of "knowing why", or perhaps we should say *remembering* why. Remembering why we reorganised our working tasks, why we bought that ICT system, why one project failed or the other succeeded. "Knowing how" was also referred to often, however this definition does not really convey the importance of what we found. Of course, our interviewees knew how to do their jobs and many other things as well, but they knew how to do their jobs in more than one way. "Know-who" was very important to many of our interviewees, indeed almost everyone we spoke to mentioned the importance of conferring with colleagues, not only to get information from them as Lundvall suggests, but also to discuss alternatives with them or to share tasks with them. We also found examples of "knowing what" and we assume that much of this is based on formal education or subsequent training. We did however find some examples which might be better classified as "remembering what", such as remembering where the cables under the building go, when the drawings have been lost. When focusing on the age or long experience of the people in our case studies, many nuances of Lundvall's model became evident which are not explicitly present in the model. We also found that some of the forms of knowing, suggested by Antonacopoulou (2006) helped us to describe and understand what our interviewees were telling us. "Knowing by storing and by repeating", featured strongly in our cases. We found this to be typical of practice-based learning over time where the old ways of doing things were stored and compared with the new ones and repetitive activities were fine-tuned over time to become an integrated part of the individual's repertoire. We also found examples of knowing by reflecting, questioning, synthesising and improvising.

Perhaps the most valuable knowledge we found among our over 50s, was what we could classify as situated knowledge, indeed much of what we have defined as senior competence may have limited value outside their current work situation. This might be the ability to deal with a particular type of situation such as an organisation which is not following the rules or how to know whose best practice really is the best, based on past experience or how to communicate complex information to a particular group of people. We also observed that the experiences which shaped this learning were often specific to one organisation or one workplace and were often developed to counteract some weakness, such as a badly functioning ICT system, or lack of resources.

Not everyone interviewed was a member of a profession, but we found that their descriptions of how they worked bore a close resemblance to Eraut's (2000) descriptions of how professionals learn, i.e. by exchanging viewpoints with colleagues or discussing previous experiences. Eraut (1994) also mentions something which we found frequently, that is, how repeated activities might result in different meanings being generated depending on the context. We did not examine relationships to formal knowledge; however, our findings confirm Eraut's observation that drawing upon practice-based experience is an important part of the skill of the experienced worker. Lastly the ability to handle non-routine situations is one of the key elements of professional knowledge, according to Eraut and this is something which we found in most of our interviews. This acceptance that many situations can be solved in multiple ways and the practice of considering the best alternative before deciding upon the action to be taken, was so common in our cases, that it was considered a normal part of everyday work, considered so normal that they were barely aware of it. Indeed, this match between Eraut's descriptions of professionals and the cases discussed in this paper, leads us to wonder if many of Eraut's professionals were perhaps also over 50.

These ways of describing adult competence and learning in the workplace go a long way in explaining our main findings however, we have not found an accepted concept which includes some of the wider aspects we have observed as an important part of being an older worker. The kind of competence identified in the cases in the current study is similar in many ways to earlier research. However, our focus on age has provided us with examples which exhibit particular aspects of knowledge and our analysis suggests that they demonstrate related, but more nuanced examples than earlier research. In our analysis we used the idea of age or maturity to explain some of the findings, we will now elaborate on this.

Older workers have knowledge and competence necessary to do their job. They have the advantage of experience, which strengthens their ability to take decisions, reflect on alternatives, inspire colleagues and perform their job in cooperation with others. They have learned and developed ways to do their job that allow them to act with less preparation and almost without conscious thoughts. They know how to do their work without having to think about how they know it. In addition, they use their age and maturity to achieve results and interact successfully with others, such as colleagues, managers or the recipients of the services the workplace provides. They are more than competent old workers; they are what we define as *wise workers*.

Wisdom is often connected to old age. "Old and wise", as the saying goes. Edmondson (2015) discusses how "the idea of wisdom was seen as offering a goal for developing and changing during the lifecourse that was independent of direct involvement in types of work that depended on physical fitness" (2015: 156). This reminds us of our interviewees who talked about "working smarter, not harder". In a different project (Hilsen & Strand, 2006) a kindergarten director talked about women in their 60s still working with the children. As she described it (in personal communication): "They don't climb trees as well as their younger colleagues, but they can talk the children down from the trees". Using experience and competence to do the job in spite of possible physical limitations can also be seen as an aspect of wisdom.

Although there is no generally accepted definition of wisdom, Edmondson (2015: 164) sorts theories of wisdom according to whether there is a tolerance of lack of perfection or not, and whether wisdom is seen as interpersonal as opposed to exclusively individual or not. According to this model of discriminating among theories of wisdom, there are "distinctions between wisdom envisaged as an extraordinary perfection and in more attainable versions, or between wisdom as reached in isolation and wisdom reached in some form of connection with others" (ibid.). We would place our wise workers in the lower perfection quadrant, in Edmondson's model, i.e. they can be described as wise without having achieved perfection in their demonstration of wisdom. We would also define wisdom of the wise worker as interpersonal, that is related to social interaction with others.

Another distinction in theories of wisdom is between those who see wisdom as a set of skills, wisdom as expertise (Baltes and colleagues referred to as the Berlin Wisdom Paradigm) and those that see wisdom as a particular personal characteristic (Ardelt, 2004; Baltes & Staudinger, 2000; Edmondson, 2015; Gugerell & Riffert, 2012).

The Berlin Wisdom Paradigm sets out criteria that define wisdom as a type of expertise. "Probably most important for a clarification of the explicit definitions are the five criteria of wisdom-related knowledge: (a) rich factual knowledge, (b) rich procedural knowledge, (c) life span contextualism, (d) relativism, and (e) uncertainty" (Gugerell & Riffert,

2012: 227–228). While the first two criteria are "characteristic of all types of expertise and stem from the tradition of research in expertise" (Baltes & Staudinger, 2000: 125), the latter three are "meta-criteria that in their separate and joint expression, we consider specific for wisdom" (ibid.).

On the other hand, Ardelt defines wisdom as a composite of cognitive, reflective and affective qualities (Ardelt, 1997: 15). She argues that the cognitive dimension of wisdom refers to the cognitive ability to see truth as it is, not clouded by wishes and desires. While this element is important, it depends on the reflective component of wisdom, that allows us to reflect on what we see without being influenced by subjectivity and projections. Lastly, she argues for the affective component of wisdom, making the person able to develop compassion for others. As described: "Having overcome all their projections, reduced their self-centeredness, and gained a deeper insight into their own and others' motives and behavior, they are able to develop feelings of genuine empathy, sympathy, and compassion for others" (Ardelt, 2000: 361). In several studies (Ardelt, 1997, 2000) she explores how this wisdom depends on social and psychological resources and assets early in life, and finds that wisdom predicts life satisfaction in old age.

As we see from the above discussion, some of the literature on wisdom and old age seem to see meaning and wisdom as an individual coping with life at an existential level, while others focus on wisdom as a set of skills, what we can call *contextual wisdom*, wisdom as performance of wisdom in settings, such as worklife. In our understanding of wisdom, we do not reject the understanding of wisdom as a result of individual coping with life. Our wise workers demonstrate life wisdom, in their stories of acceptance of their stage in life, compassion for younger colleagues and willingness to share their knowledge. When they talk about being more tolerant as grandmothers than they were as mothers, this reflects their individual journey through life. In many ways this reminds us of Erik Erikson's description of human development stages from infancy to end of life (Erikson, 1963), where his eighth, as last, stage covers the age from around 65 years. This phase has the goal of attaining ego integrity, described as "realising the continuity in one's own personality and one's meaning for others" (Edmondson, 2015: 39). The basic virtue resulting from successfully achieving ego integrity, according to Erikson, is wisdom (McLeod, 2018).

At the same time our main focus is on how this wisdom is expressed in the way they talk about and perform their work. The wise worker is wise from a long work career, learning and reflecting on work, as they perform their everyday activities in the workplace.

A different take on the discussion of wisdom and ageing can be found with the American philosopher Martha Nussbaum. Nussbaum (2011) has developed theory of justice and entitlement for humans that define and compare quality of life at both individual and societal level, expressed through ten central capabilities. This theory combines individual conditions with societal conditions, and thus bridges the gap between the individual and the society in which the individual lives. Quality of life in old age (and being able to live to an old age) is covered in several of these capabilities. "… a decent political order must secure to all citizens at least a threshold level of these ten Central Capabilities:

1. *Life*. Being able to live to the end of a human life of normal length; not dying prematurely, or before one's life is so reduced as to be not worth living.
2. *Bodily Health*. Being able to have good health, including reproductive health; to be adequately nourished; to have adequate shelter.
3. *Bodily Integrity*. Being able to move freely from place to place; to be secure against violent assault, including sexual assault and domestic violence; having opportunities for sexual satisfaction and for choice in matters of reproduction.
4. *Senses, Imagination, and Thought*. Being able to use the senses, to imagine, think, and reason—and to do these things in a "truly human" way, a way informed and cultivated by an adequate education, including, but by no means limited to, literacy and basic mathematical and scientific training. Being able to use imagination and thought in connection with experiencing and producing works and events of one's own choice, religious, literary, musical, and so forth. Being able to use one's mind in ways protected by guarantees of freedom of expression with respect to both political and artistic speech, and freedom of religious exercise. Being able to have pleasurable experiences and to avoid non-beneficial pain.
5. *Emotions*. Being able to have attachments to things and people outside ourselves; to love those who love and care for us, to grieve at their absence; in general, to love, to grieve, to experience longing, gratitude, and justified anger. Not having one's emotional

development blighted by fear and anxiety. (Supporting this capability means supporting forms of human association that can be shown to be crucial in their development.)

6. *Practical Reason.* Being able to form a conception of the good and to engage in critical reflection about the planning of one's life. (This entails protection for the liberty of conscience and religious observance.)
7. *Affiliation.* (A) Being able to live with and toward others, to recognize and show concern for other humans, to engage in various forms of social interaction; to be able to imagine the situation of another. (Protecting this capability means protecting institutions that constitute and nourish such forms of affiliation, and also protecting the freedom of assembly and political speech.) (B) Having the social bases of self-respect and non-humiliation; being able to be treated as a dignified being whose worth is equal to that of others. This entails provisions of non-discrimination on the basis of race, sex, sexual orientation, ethnicity, caste, religion, national origin and species.
8. *Other Species.* Being able to live with concern for and in relation to animals, plants, and the world of nature.
9. *Play.* Being able to laugh, to play, to enjoy recreational activities.
10. *Control over one's Environment.* (A) Political. Being able to participate effectively in political choices that govern one's life; having the right of political participation, protections of free speech and association. (B) Material. Being able to hold property (both land and movable goods), and having property rights on an equal basis with others; having the right to seek employment on an equal basis with others; having the freedom from unwarranted search and seizure. In work, being able to work as a human, exercising practical reason and entering into meaningful relationships of mutual recognition with other workers" (Nussbaum, 2011: 33–34).

Our mature workers live a long life with health sufficient to work. They express positive and—sometimes—negative emotions and affiliation towards their co-workers and the users of their services. Wisdom is developed through relationships with others during a long career, and practical reason is expressed in critical reflection about their work and life.

On the individual level, the central capabilities (ibid.) describe a level of quality of life that we recognize in the stories from our interviewees.

As described in our cases, they have lived and learned through a long working career, and this achieved wisdom is expressed in their descriptions of how they perform their job in connection to and in relationship with co-workers and users of the services.

By adding a discussion on wisdom to our discussion of the kind of competence which our older employees have, we move beyond conventional understandings of competence. Our wise worker is competent in the ways we have described, but they have also lived a long life and aged, like a good wine. They have mellowed with age, and they exemplify this by referring to personal characteristics, like being more tolerant and accepting of others than when they were younger. They have learned to accept that we all make mistakes sometimes, and how to go on in spite of mistakes. They belong to a generation that shares cultural and political references and can relate to others through such shared references. These additional sides to senior competence, which are not normally defined as competence, make us look for a broader concept, and the literature on wisdom emboldened us to include these additional characteristics and define our workers as wise workers. Whereas the literature on wisdom often relates its discussions to the field of psychology and philosophy, we were inspired by the concept of wisdom to enrich our discussion on senior competence in the workplace. We understand wisdom to be a wider concept than competence when describing our older workers.

The wise worker is a mature, older worker who uses their age and many years of experience in working life to do their job in a way that benefits themselves, their co-workers and the organisation where they work. They are wise workers. We summarise the qualities of the wise worker in the following list:

The Wise Worker

Knows how (exactly how)

- Knows who
- Remembers why
- Is a translator and bridge builder
- Creates a safe environment
- Embodies authority
- Shares knowledge
- Carries organisational history
- Is selective

References

Aasheim, C., Shropshire, J., Li, L., & Kadlec, C. (2012). Knowledge and skill requirements for entry-level IT workers: A longitudinal study. *J Info Syst Edu, 23*(2), 193.

Antonacopoulou, E. (2006). Modes of knowing in practice: The relationship between knowledge and learning revisited. In B. Renzl, K. Matzler, & H. Hinterhuber (Eds.), *The future of knowledge management*. Palgrave Macmillan.

Ardelt, M. (1997). Wisdom and life satisfaction in old age. *Journal of Gerontology, Psychological Sciences, 52B*(1), 15–27.

Ardelt, M. (2000). Antecedents and effects of wisdom in old age. In *Research on aging, 22*(4 July 2000), 360–394.

Ardelt, M. (2004). Wisdom as expert knowledge system: A critical review of a contemporary operationalization of an ancient concept. *Human Development, 47*(5), 257–285. https://doi.org/10.1159/000079154.

Baltes, P. B., & Staudinger, U. (2000). Wisdom: A metaheuristic (pragmatic) to orchestrate mind and virtue toward excellence. *American Psychologist, 55*(1), 122–136.

Edmondson, R. (2015). *Ageing, insight and wisdom: Meaning and practice across the lifecourse*. Policy Press.

Eraut, M. (1994). *Developing professional knowledge and competence*.

Eraut, M. (2000). Non-formal learning and professional knowledge at work. *British Journal of Educational Psychology, 70*(Pt 1)(1), 113–136.

Erikson, E. H. (1963). *Childhood and society*. Norton.

Gugerell, S., & Riffert, F. (2012). On defining "Wisdom": Baltes, Ardelt, Ryan, and Whitehead. *Interchange, 42/3,* 225–259, 2011. Springer 2012. https://evidencebasedwisdom.com/2015/09/20/the-berlin-wisdom-paradigm-an-expert-knowledge-system/.

Hilsen, A. I., & Strand, B. E. (Eds.). (2006). *Fortellinger om å få det til. AFI-publikasjoner*. Arbeidsforskningsinstituttet.

Lundvall, B. Å. (1996). The Social Dimension of the Learning Economy. DRUID Working Papers 96-1, DRUID, Copenhagen Business School, Department of Industrial Economics and Strategy/Aalborg University, Department of Business Studies.

Lundvall, B.-Å., & Johnson, B. (1994). The learning economy. *Journal of Industry Studies, 1, Nr., 2,* 23–42.

McLeod, S. A. (2018, May 3). *Erik Erikson's stages of psychosocial development*. Simply Psychology. https://www.simplypsychology.org/Erik-Erikson.html.

Nussbaum, M. (2011). *Creating capabilities: The human development approach* (pp. 33–34). Harvard University Press.

CHAPTER 8

Conclusions

Abstract We will discuss how the concept of the wise worker can be used in the workplace and how a focus on late career competence can be of value to employers, employees and policymakers. At the same time, it is important to acknowledge that age alone is not enough to ensure wisdom. We will set out some conditions to understanding and using the concept of the wise worker.

Keywords Wise worker · Late career competence

Over the last decades the expected life span has increased in most Western countries and the health of elders has improved significantly, opening up to the possibility of longer working careers. In recent years there has been a focus on increasing the actual retirement age among older employees, and many European countries, including Norway, have implemented extensive pension reforms. The advantage of having older workers in the workforce goes beyond the need for labour or the need for more people working and paying taxes and fewer people living on retirement benefits. The findings presented in this book, tell us about the advantages of having older workers in the labour market connected to the jobs they do and the competence and maturity they bring to those jobs.

A. I. Hilsen and D. S. Olsen, *The Importance and Value of Older Employees*, https://doi.org/10.1007/978-981-16-2861-0_8

When discussing late career competence in the workplace, it is important to acknowledge that not all older workers possess all these components. Age is no guarantee for wisdom and senior competence is *individual*, i.e. it differs from senior to senior. To develop wisdom, one needs to be constantly willing to learn and reflect on this learning. As several of our interviewees pointed out, reflection on action is a key to developing better practice, and being willing to challenge accepted practices and ways of working is a step towards developing improved practices. This is also one of the reasons why age diversity is useful. When older and experienced workers collaborate with younger colleagues fresh from the education system, experience-based knowledge has to be made explicit and explained to be shared. Building bridges between different types of knowledge and between younger and older workers help the older worker to recognise what they know and why they do things the way they do.

Another aspect of long career competence is that it is *relational*, i.e. it is demonstrated in interaction with others. Our wise workers are recognised as wise by their colleagues, managers and clients. The advantage to their organisations lies in the way they perform their work and share their knowledge in their daily work. Some of our interviewees worked as part of a team or a close-knit workgroup, such as in the hospital. Others did more solitary work, such as some of the inspectors. Although the Inspectorate had an ambition of always working in pairs when controlling an enterprise, in practice they told us that they often worked alone. Constrictions due to economy and staffing led to more solitary work than desired. In our interviews we noticed that the older employees who worked closely with colleagues could more easily describe what age and experience had taught them. They were used to having explain and share their competence, and this also promoted better recognition of this competence. The interviewees who worked alone needed more time and reflection to explain how age and experience had contributed to their competence. Working closely with colleagues enabled a better understanding of what they knew and why they performed their work the way they did.

A third important aspect of being a wise worker is that their competence is contextual, i.e. it is dependent upon the specific setting in which it is expressed. Settings are necessary to understand how the wisdom of older workers is expressed—nothing happens in a generic "workplace", but in specific workplaces with specific people doing practical work. This implies that the context should be explored and identified in each new workplace. What we have identified and described in this book is contingent on the specific workplaces we have studied. These workplaces were mainly public sector organisations and mainly large organisations and reflect the conditions there. Were we to do the same studies in different organisations, we would expect to find different examples and different stories. While the nurses talk about "the clinical eye", being able to read the situation based on long experience, we might expect to find parallels in other types of work. Once in a production factory, someone described (personal communication) how the older operators could discover when something was wrong before the alarm went off by the sound in the production facility. This "experienced ear" is dependent on long experience, and is clearly a parallel to "the clinical eye". Each type of workplace and type of work will be different. Further studies would be necessary to explore and illuminate the characteristics of the wise worker in other sectors and workplaces. Indeed, new studies might expand our concept of the wise worker.

Different workplaces can be influenced by managers and how they encourage or exclude the older employees from new ways of working and new learning. Not only can management behaviour reduce learning opportunities, but also signal a lack of confidence in older employees. The process of deskilling and demotivation has been described as a "senior syndrome" by The Centre for Senior Policy (www.seniorpolitikk.no). This process is characterised by managers who have declining expectations of their senior staff, leading to fewer challenges and professional offers for older employees. This in turn results in declining expectations and motivation among the employees themselves, thus leading to less renewal and professional development. This situation can then exacerbate the managers' declining expectations. This is a negative spiral of expectations and development, which means that the older workers are neither seen as an asset to the organisation nor encouraged to develop and use their competence. There is no reason to believe that this senior syndrome is specific to Norway and we would expect to find similar situations in other countries.

For long career competence to be of use in the labour market and be an advantage to employers, there are some important considerations. We started this book with a story from one of our case organisations, the high-ranking manager who was challenged by the Board to define the value and potential of older employees and any particular knowledge or contributions they could make. This points to a major consideration:

Long career competence must be defined in relation to the workplace in which it is expressed, described in relation to the performance of the work operations interacting with colleagues, clients and others. When exploring this type of competence, one will find that not all older workers perform in the same way. The competence is individual, and some older workers will excel in some ways and others in other ways. Also not all older workers will be wise and mature. Age in itself is not a guarantee for wisdom. This means that an organisation that wants to explore the competence of their older employees must stop and ask how age and experience make these particular employees, in this particular workplace, more valuable. Our experiences showed us that the question of how age and experience contribute to the work performance of older workers, triggered engaging and positive discussions. Once a description of senior competence has been produced in a particular organisation, then the employer can take steps to support and encourage all its older employees to develop this kind of competence. Senior competence must be identified based on the specific work carried out and the groups of workers. When recognised, measures to support and develop such competence can then be incorporated in human resource management procedures of the organisation.

Having reached an understanding of the contribution of mature older workers, the organisation should strive to make sure this competence is being used and shared among employees. As pointed out, senior competence is relational, and it is in use one sees the value of the seniors' competence. Knowledge can be individual and passive, but competence is what is used to achieve results and solve tasks. Thus, seniors must be challenged, encouraged and involved in workplace activities. Although the situation in Norway, as described in the introduction, is fairly age positive with policy initiatives and incentives to promote longer careers, there are, as in other countries, still obstacles and negative attitudes to overcome.

When describing senior competence and its value, this has been done in relation to the local situation in the specific organisation. We have also highlighted the importance of viewing this competence as something closely bound to the organisation and situation in which it developed. This should not, however, limit the concept of the wise worker to these specific cases, or indeed to Norway. Any modern workplace with employees who have long experience will probably be able to find wise workers and examples of senior competence. The competence of these workers and its value will be different due to differences in local and national conditions.

We argue that exploring what long career competence looks like in the individual workplace, is the foundation for recognition and further development of the employees' competence. Once managers and the organisations recognise and value long career competence, they need to organise work so that this competence can be shared. The value of age diversity lies in complementarity, that the elderly and experienced possess some types of expertise, while the young enter the workplace with their different skills. As one older interviewee said:

> *I also do not expect blind admiration from younger colleagues, but I will be happy if they value things that I have experienced and that can come in handy for them.*

Senior competence must be shared to be valuable for the organisation as a whole, and facilitating collaboration and experience sharing across age groups supports this. It may be done through mentorship schemes, sponsorship and "shoulder-to-shoulder training", but it is equally important to think about age diversity when assembling project teams, teams and work teams.

This book has explored and identified how the wise worker functions in an efficient way and how she or he utilises his or her knowledge and experience in an appropriate way. The practice of the wise worker deserves to be recognised and valued by employers and employees alike.

The manufacturer's authorised representative in the EU is Springer Nature Customer Service Centre GmbH, Europaplatz 3, 69115 Heidelberg, Germany. If you have any concerns regarding our products, please contact ProductSafety@springernature.com

Printed and bound by CPI Group (UK) Ltd, Croydon, CR0 4YY
30/09/2026
02225264-0001